THE DARK SIDE
OF FAITH

don't waste your pain

Doug Bergsma

Next Step Books

God Bless You

Doug Bergsma

The Dark Side of Faith
don't waste your pain

Cover by Nick Delliskave
Cover Design by Emily Lindsey

Library of Congress Control Number: 2015916666

ISBN-13: 978-1-937671-28-0
ISBN-10: 1937671283

Dedication

I would like to dedicate this book in the loving memory of my mother, the fiercest, most spot-on theologian I have ever met. I have very seldom encountered anyone who more intensely studied and lived the Word of God than she did. Much of the good I have been able to do in ministry and in exposition of God's Word (by God's grace), I attribute to her.

Acknowledgments

My deepest appreciation to...

All those who labored with us in prayer and on the project—along with providing much encouragement—to bring this book to completion. I would like to give a special thanks to Brian Mannor and Trish Konieczny for the hours of advice, editing, and just plain putting up with me. A special thanks to Steve, Dustin, Judy, Beverly, Linda, and basically everyone on my staff for letting me rant and brainstorm about this project. I probably drove half of you crazy. I would like to give a special thanks also to Emily Lindsey, for designing the cover of this book.

I want to thank my wife Caryn for encouraging me, and putting up with my endless daydreaming and staring off into space, completely disconnected from the family or the moment, all due to being pregnant with this book.

Lastly, and most importantly, I would like to thank the Lord for His grace in my life and the privilege of allowing me to share some of the lessons I have learned with you.

Table of Contents

Foreword

In *The Dark Side of Faith*, Doug Bergsma shares not only his own journey of faith—which is a story of terrible tragedy and tremendous triumph—but also how you can grab hold of the victory in your own difficult circumstances. When my wife and I read the book together, it moved us greatly and inspired our faith in God.

When tragedy or great difficulties strike, many run from God and shipwreck their lives and sometimes their whole family; Doug ran and experienced victory after victory as God met him and turned what the devil meant for evil into good.

I've been a close personal friend of Doug's since our college years. I remember when each of the tragic events he writes about took place. And, I can attest that the godly principles he writes about in these pages really were applied in his life at those very moments. Because of the wise choices he made and that he shares in this book, he has come through those dark times victorious. Doug is truly a person of faith. I'm glad he wrote this book to help show others how to be the same.

Duane Vander Klok
Lead Pastor, Resurrection Life Church
Grandville, MI

Introduction

A s you begin reading this book, there are several things in the forefront of my mind that I would like to share with you. To begin with, in spite of its title, this is not a dark, morbid book that soaks in pain, trouble, and trials. Rather, it is an exciting glimpse into the spiritual realm behind the scenes in our everyday lives that helps us to more clearly see who God is and what He has in mind for us as He orchestrates His eternal plan. He does this by strategically involving Himself in the day-to-day events that occur in our personal lives. Our storyline shows God's intimate involvement with us, right down to the smallest detail. Nothing is lost or wasted in the building of His kingdom. Everything God does is for His purpose and for our ultimate good as well. He uses everything—both the good and bad—our trouble, pain, and tragedy: even our failures and mistakes. It is very important that we recognize, understand, and cooperate with God's plan for us. Why? Because there is a tremendous spiritual battle being waged behind the scenes over our life's purpose. The enemy wants to create both real and phantom offenses that separate us from God. He wants to knock us off-course so that we do not fulfill our life's purpose. As you read, it is my prayer that you will clearly recognize the tactics the enemy uses to invade a person's thought life and literally hijack their free will and ultimately shipwreck their faith. Rather than simply discuss the potential for disaster, though, we will actually concentrate on **the one key thing** that we can both embrace and do, that will make it possible for us to overcome every obstacle and come out a winner every time, no matter what the situation or the circumstances we may find ourselves in.

In the latter part of the book, I spend a good deal of time sharing some important things that need to be in place if we are to survive and actually thrive in any situation we might find ourselves in. Also, throughout the book, I share some unique and sometimes crazy stories from my own life and from the experiences of others that I hope will help you better navigate your own life and circumstances.

I think it is somewhat ironic that I am writing a book with this grim-sounding title, because if you knew me, you would know that I am one of the most happy, fun loving, and positive people you could ever run into. In light of this fact, I promise that, as you read, several very powerful things will happen. You will not feel dragged down by what I share with you; rather, you will actually identify with a number of the stories and lessons shared in this book. Further, I hope you will be substantially encouraged and motivated as you read. It is also my prayer that in these pages you will find fresh faith and courage to press on with your life with all of your might. Lastly, as I prayed over this book and its contents, I received a strong impression from the Holy Spirit that He is going to speak to you about your life beyond the pages of this book, and give you fresh revelation, direction, and strength to run your course and go the distance. God bless you as you read!

Pastor Doug
The Dark Side of Faith

Chapter I – The Job Factor

I was numb. It was like a dream. I hung up the phone and stared out the front store window at two police officers walking across the street. A dispatcher had just informed me on the phone that they were coming. She also informed me that my wife, Barbara, and my youngest daughter, Joanna, had been in a serious car accident. The reality of what had happened hit me before the officers actually told me that they were gone. They had been instantly killed in a violent, three-car accident. Suddenly, what I had been feeling made sense. About three hours before, a feeling came over me that was hard to describe. It was an emptiness, and the feeling of being lost and without direction. Now, I realized that I had actually felt them being taken from me.

For 20 years, Barbara and I had been one in every sense of the word. I remember that God moment when He directed me to go to Christ for the Nations Institute in Dallas, Texas, because He had a wife for me there.

Barb had been the first girl I met when I walked onto campus with my friend, Duane Vander Klok. She was 20 years old, and as it turned out, she was the Assistant Dean of Women. I was impressed. I remember asking a staff member how someone so young had risen to such a lofty position. The reply, "If you want to find Barbara, she's in the prayer room." Say no more! God had sent me there. She was a beautiful and classy girl who prayed, and God knew I needed that! I was not worthy. I fell in love almost at first sight. I asked her out, and I will never forget coming home that night from our first date. As I stepped into the room, my friend Duane's voice came from the dark and asked me, "So, is she the one?" I said, "Yes she is." Six weeks later, I asked her to marry me. I was so love-struck and infatuated that one night I woke up dreaming that Barbara was in my roommate Duane's bed. I thought there would be no harm in giving her a little kiss. So, I got up and I went over to the bed and stooped over. When I hit the mustache, I knew I was making a terrible mistake. Duane woke up spitting and swinging. We laugh about it to this day.

Needless to say, Barbara and I were married right after graduation. Duane also met his wife, Jeanne, at Christ for the Nations Institute. After they were married, they went to Mexico as missionaries. As for me, I resumed my former position as a worship leader, Bible teacher, and elder at Maranatha Ministries in Grandville, Michigan. Barb and I went on to have a dream marriage, and we had five beautiful children: three sons and two daughters. Life was sweet. It literally could not have been better.

The Domino Effect

Now, that relationship was over in the blink of an eye. On top of that, my little ten-year-old Joanna, the sweetest little girl on the planet, was gone as well. It was pure pain! I did not know how to miss them or grieve individually over them. I couldn't separate them. It was just a big lump of pain and emptiness.

That evening, my three sons, Cal, Jonathan, and Daniel, as well as my remaining daughter, Carly, sat numbly together at our home as other family members and friends came in to offer condolences and comfort. The local Christian radio station, WJQ, launched community-wide prayer support for our family. Days later, thousands of people came to the funeral home to comfort and be with us. To this day, I am amazed by the outpouring of love we received from the entire community. My heart goes out to those who do not have that kind of support.

The grace of God carried my family and me, and the prayers of so many brought a divine numbness that took the sharp edge off of the pain we were feeling. I'll never forget standing with my boys and my daughter in the cemetery and laying my hand on the two caskets, saying goodbye for the last time. Then we drove away and left them there, along with a piece of our lives. It seemed so wrong, so brutal; I remember being all but blinded by tears. And then it was over just as suddenly as it had happened. All the crowds of sympathizers, the letters and cards, and most of all, my Lady and my little 10 year old, JoJo, were gone, all gone. I'll also never forget the feeling of walking into my bedroom the night of the funeral and staring at the huge, empty bed. It looked stark, a visible reflection of the hole in my soul. I took a double dose of NyQuil® Nighttime Cold Formula, crawled into bed, pulled out my Bible and opened it. The only thing I could think of that I could relate to in my condition was the Bible character of Job. I remembered the fact that he was one of the most notable men in the East: popular, well to do, with a big family. But then, like me and worse—in the twinkling of an eye his whole world collapsed and it went downhill from there. Right then and there, I decided to immerse myself in the story of Job and try to find some truth, comfort, and direction: anything that could help me get through it all...then the NyQuil took effect, and I drifted off to sleep.

For the next few days, I immersed myself in the story of Job and his journey from a dream life into a world of pain. Meanwhile, my own life and family continued to be rocked by many painful changes. I found out that my 16 year old daughter, Carly, had an intense argument with her Mom and yelled at her little sister the day that they were killed. In her grief and pain, Carly had written a letter to both of them, asking forgiveness and telling them she loved them. She slipped her personal letter to each of them into their caskets. But alas, her pain didn't subside. She cried herself to sleep every night for nearly a year. On top of that, she got angry with God and herself, and she fell away from faith and went as far away from God as she could get. In short order, she left home and moved into an apartment in another town. As time went by, she dabbled in the occult, drugs, alcohol, immorality: anything to dull the sense of pain, anger, and loss in her soul. I'll get back to more of Carly's story a bit later.

Meanwhile, my youngest son, Daniel, who was only 13 years old, had lost his Mom and sister, the latter of whom was his best friend. Daniel and Joanna were home-schooled by their Mom, and every day when I went to work, I would see my beautiful little trio doing school around the table, along with Shammy, our small beagle, who would always sit near them, wagging his tail. Even Shammy had been killed in the accident. They had been taking him to the vet the day the accident occurred. Daniel was so lost. I would hear him sobbing in his bed at night and early in the mornings. Hearing that little guy sobbing tore my heart even worse. I would have done anything to take away his pain. Within a very short time period follow-ing the accident, each of my two oldest sons, Cal and Jonathan, got married, and I found myself alone in a big house, with only a very sad little boy, in the middle of nowhere. My beautiful family of seven had dwindled down to two very sad people.

At this point, life had lost its luster for me. I had a beautiful home in the country, an SUV, a sports car, a boat, etc., but the very sight or thought of those things made me feel sick and hollow. I came to the fresh realization that relationships with friends and loved ones are everything, and without someone to share them with, stuff means less than nothing. Life suddenly felt very strange. I was single, alone, and after having been married for 20 years, I only knew how to act married. I continued to go out with my married friends, but it wasn't the same. I felt like a completely different person than who I had been. I was swimming in a private world of loss, pain, and loneliness.

Looking for Answers

There was only one thing that kept me on track during this period. It was the same thing that kept Job on track in his time of struggle and loss. That one thing was that I clung to God and chose to believe that no matter what happened, or why it happened, or who was responsible, I would trust God, and I would believe that His words were and are true. He said in Romans 8:28 (NKJV), "And we know that all things work together for good to those who love God, to those who are called according to His purpose." I believe that my decision to trust God—no matter what—was an important one. Over the years, I had seen many people hit a tough period in their lives, and when things began to fall apart, they became offended. They started to listen to the lies of Satan, who desperately wants to separate us from God's grace and our purpose. That silent, accusing voice would inject thoughts and doubts about God into a person's mind, saying things like, "God isn't listening to your prayers…maybe He's not there at all!" Or, "If He was, why would He let that happen to you and yours?" Deep down, I knew that none of those things were true. I had the blessing of being taught the truth from the Word of God beginning at a very young age. Beneath all of the pain, I still understood that God is in control. He has a master plan for every one of His children; He hears every prayer, and there is a reason for everything that happens. Far beyond the specific circumstances that we encounter, there is something immense going on behind the scenes of this life. That is one of my primary reasons for writing this book, and as you keep reading, it is my prayer that you will find that many of the things I have discovered will begin to make sense in the context of your life as well.

Up to this time of crisis, I had generally acknowledged—and had actually known beyond any doubt—that God was in control of my life. I knew the Bible said that every hair on my head is numbered and that God values me (and you) beyond any other part of His creation. I knew He had my ultimate welfare at stake as well, but I was now on a journey through a very dark corridor of my life. I desperately wanted to have a greater understanding of what was happening, and why.

Chapter 2 - The Cosmic Wager

As I continued to read the story of Job, I became re-acquainted with his position as a very wealthy, very happy, very well-to-do man; one of the richest men in the Middle East. He had a big, beautiful family. On top of all this, Job had a very good relationship with God; he loved God; he worshiped God. He even sacrificed offerings and prayed for each one of his children, just to cover them with God's grace in case one of them was doing something wrong. This man had it all, and he had it all covered. He was doing everything right. But suddenly, the story took on a very interesting twist. It switched in focus from the physical world we all live in to the spiritual world. It showed a scene where God was in some sort of executive meeting with His angels, and then who shows up? The prince of darkness himself, Satan. I felt expectation growing as I read the story. I was going to get a look at what was going on in the spiritual world, behind the scene of Job's misfortune. Maybe it would shed some light on my situation.

During this chapter, it may seem as though I am leaving my personal storyline to switch gears and focus on something else: my insights from Job. It is imperative that I do so briefly, in order to lay a foundation for the things that I want to share in the chapters ahead. The lessons I learned from studying Job have played a huge role in helping me through the most difficult period of my life, which I just told you about in Chapter 1. During that terrible time, I gained a much greater understanding of God and His ways, and a much greater understanding of the tactics Satan uses to derail us and ruin our lives. In spite of all I was going through at that time, I emerged from my study of Job with fresh hope, along with divine energy for my life and future. We will get back to my story shortly, but for a moment, let's step back and look at Job's story. Let's look behind the scenes into the invisible world and listen in on the conversation between God and Satan concerning Job, exactly as it is recorded in the pages of God's Word.

Job 1:6-12 (NIV)

[6]One day the angels came to present themselves before the Lord, and Satan also came with them.

[7]The Lord said to Satan, "Where have you come from?" Satan answered the Lord, "From roaming throughout the earth, going back and forth on it."

[8]Then the Lord said to Satan, "Have you considered my servant Job? There is no one on earth like him; he is blameless and upright, a man who fears God and shuns evil."

[9]"Does Job fear God for nothing?" Satan replied. [10]"Have you not put a hedge around him and his household and everything he has? You have blessed the work of his hands, so that his flocks and herds are spread throughout the land. [11]But now stretch out your

hand and strike everything he has, and he will surely curse you to your face."

¹²The Lord said to Satan, "Very well, then, everything he has is in your power, but on the man himself do not lay a finger."

The Wager is On

This portion of Scripture presents a truly amazing picture. What in the world?!! A gigantic cosmic wager between God and Satan, the point of interest—Job—and the quality of his relationship with God.

In this story, God gives us an unparalleled look into the spiritual realm. We get a glimpse at what goes on behind the scenes. I believe that one of God's main intents in all of this, was that we would see and understand just how important our lives and our everyday decisions really are. Also, I think this story gives us real insight about Satan's tactics and how he works in any way he can to separate us from God, from His grace, and ultimately, from our purpose and destiny.

As we first see Satan appearing among the angels in some kind of executive gathering with God, it seems surprising that he would have access to this type of meeting. The Bible emphatically states that at an earlier time, before man was created, Satan had rebelled against God with one-third of the angels and was ejected from heaven (Isaiah 14:12-15 and Revelation 12:4.) Satan then set up a rival Kingdom in the heavenlies, sometimes referred to as the "second heaven," between God's dwelling place and earth. In Ephesians 2:1-2 (NKJV), the Bible calls him the "prince of the power of the air ... who now works in the sons of disobedience." However, he is also called the "accuser of our brethren, who accused them before our God day and night" (Revelation 12:10, NKJV.) To do this, he must have had some kind of access to God. It should be noted that this encounter between God and Satan concerning Job was before the redemptive time of Christ's Advent—His birth, His life, and His atoning death. At the cross, Jesus paid for our sins and canceled Satan's legal claims over the human race. Colossians 2:14 (ISV) states, "having erased the charges that were brought against us, along with their obligations that were hostile to us. He took those charges away when he nailed them to the cross. And when he had disarmed the rulers and the authorities, he made a public spectacle of them, triumphing over them in the cross." This victory over Satan and payment for our sin made it possible for all men and women to have a relationship with God and a clean slate based on what Christ has done for them.

Back to Job's story. God asks Satan what he's been up to (as if He didn't know). Satan says he's been going to and fro on the earth, which basically implied that Satan had been observing all the good things God was accomplishing, and was doing his best to wreck and destroy those very things.

God then brought up Job and said, "Have you noticed Job? He's a real good man, an awesome man who loves me and serves me completely of his own free will" (Job 1:8.) Satan then launched into what he does best. He questioned God concerning the quality of Job's relationship with God and tried to cast a seed of doubt about how God got such a quality commitment from Job. By the way, this is the main tactic Satan has used from the beginning of time. It worked with Eve in the garden, and now he was trying it on the God of the universe. If he could separate Job from God through lies and circumstance, he could prove that God's whole process of ever developing a real, working love relationship with the human race was flawed. Beyond that, if he could keep God from accomplishing something He wanted to do, it would mean that God was not truly God. It would show that Satan had power to stop God in some regard. This would strengthen his position and weaken God's sovereign, seemingly all-powerful control of the universe.

At this juncture, I must point out that the Bible says that God is omnipotent (all powerful), omniscient (all knowing), and omnipresent (everywhere present); He is perfectly pure, holy, righteous, and unchangeable. I love the portion of the book of Isaiah that states how big God is. Look at how God views us and the universe, in His own words:

Isaiah 40:21-22 & 25-26 (ESV)

21 Do you not know? Do you not hear?
Has it not been told you from the beginning?
Have you not understood from the foundations of the earth?

22 It is He who sits above the circle of the earth,
and its inhabitants are like grasshoppers;
who stretches out the heavens like a curtain,
and spreads them like a tent to dwell in;

25 To whom then will you compare me,
that I should be like him? says the Holy One.

26 Lift up your eyes on high and see:
who created these?
He who brings out their host by number,
calling them all by name,
by the greatness of His might,
and because He is strong in power
not one is missing.

This passage gives some specifics about what it means when we say that God is omnipotent! He is universally supreme, and His righteousness and His Word are incapable of failing in any way. On the other hand, Satan and his cohorts are spiritually dead, and despite being ejected from Heaven and defeated at the cross, the Kingdom of Darkness rages against God and His creation, looking for a weak spot: looking to steal, kill, and destroy (see John 10:10).

Satan Sees an Opportunity

As the conversation between God and Satan continued, I must imagine that Satan saw the opportunity of the ages. God was actually directly challenging him, questioning him concerning Job. Satan's tactic had always been to question God and to get us to question God concerning His dealings with us. Now, God was using the same tactic and questioning Satan and his process. God said, "Have you considered my servant Job? He's really good and he loves and serves Me of his own free will." Satan saw his opportunity in the question. God was challenging him, but He was including His relationship with Job in the mix. Satan probably couldn't believe his ears. He knew he could not overcome God outright, but now God had seemingly made Himself somewhat vulnerable by including Job in the challenge. All he had to do was drive a wedge between Job and God and get Job to doubt God and His faithfulness. If he could get Job to doubt God's goodness and faithfulness and get him to choose to abandon serving God, he could prove God was wrong about Job. He could prove that his way was greater than God's way. He could prove that he could stop the will of God from happening. And so, the cosmic wager, a wager of epic proportions, came into being.

God asked the first question, but Satan made the wager. He responded to God's question and said, "Does Job serve God for nothing? Good grief, look what you've given him—he's the richest man in the East. Anybody would serve you if you gave them that much *stuff*! Take it all away so that he has nothing, and he will curse you and abandon his relationship with you."

Before we continue with Job's story and then get back to mine (and ultimately, yours), let me restate the real issues at stake in this epic, cosmic wager between God and Satan. In this story, Job actually represents the entire human race, including you and me. Job's life became a testing ground, designed to show whose plan would succeed in captivating the heart, soul, mind, will, and emotions of the human race: God's plan or Satan's. I realized as I read through Job's story that my life—and, for that matter, everyone's life—is a testing ground with that same gigantic question hanging over it. How we answer that question will determine both the direction and quality of the life we live. God created us with a free will, and along with it a tremendous responsibility to listen to the right voice and make the right choices. God has our welfare and ultimate good in mind, but as you will see, our enemy has an entirely different agenda for our lives.

When God asked Satan, "Have you considered my servant Job?" The real issue He was addressing was His process of developing a true love relationship with men and women, a relationship based on true, pure love and loyalty. In essence, God was saying to Satan, "My process is working. True love and loyalty to Me are all evident in Job's life. I can get men and women to choose to love Me and choose right over wrong of their own free will. I can get them to deny their right to choose a self-centered existence. Once they see who I am, once they see the extent of My love for them, they will choose to love and serve Me. This will be doubly true when they see My plan for them contrasted against the wicked environment that has emerged in the wake of your fallen kingdom."

Ultimately, God was saying, "I'm working My plan on earth in the human race, pouring out all of My love, grace, and wisdom to build a real, working love relationship with human beings based on who I am and what I've done for them. You, Satan, are working your godless plan on the earth in the human race based on rebellion and self-centeredness, which basically means choosing to operate independently from Me, doing their own thing, living their lives in whatever way they please. History is revealing the horrific consequences of what happens when people choose to live independently, apart from Me. So, Satan, at your accusation and your request, I'll let you test your claims about Job. He knows Me and he loves Me. I've given him My best; now, at your request, you do your worst. Go ahead. Devise and execute the diabolical plans you have for him (with some boundaries), and we will see whose plan is working. I say I will win. My plan for humanity is the best plan. Job will choose Me and My will and My way even if he loses everything. You say 'No,' so let's find out the truth." And so it was; Satan left God's presence armed with permission to attack Job's family and estate. Shortly thereafter, all hell broke loose in Job's family and his business. I'll let you directly read the account, found in Job 1:13-19.

Job 1:13-19 (NKJV)

[13] Now there was a day when his sons and daughters were eating and drinking wine in their oldest brother's house; [14] and a messenger came to Job and said, "The oxen were plowing and the donkeys feeding beside them, [15] when the Sabeans raided them and took them away—indeed they have killed the servants with the edge of the sword; and I alone have escaped to tell you!"

[16] While he was still speaking, another also came and said, "The fire of God fell from heaven and burned up the sheep and the servants, and consumed them; and I alone have escaped to tell you!"

¹⁷ While he was still speaking, another also came and said, "The Chaldeans formed three bands, raided the camels and took them away, yes, and killed the servants with the edge of the sword; and I alone have escaped to tell you!"

¹⁸ While he was still speaking, another also came and said, "Your sons and daughters were eating and drinking wine in their oldest brother's house, ¹⁹ and suddenly a great wind came from across the wilderness and struck the four corners of the house, and it fell on the young people, and they are dead; and I alone have escaped to tell you!"

At this point, you might be starting to ask what has become a universal question. Why would the sovereign, all powerful God of the universe let all of this happen to Job? Or why, for that matter, would He let bad things happen to you, especially if the devil is behind it? Another question: if God let Satan do what he did to Job, isn't He somewhat responsible for Job's pain, and how could that be right? I know these things to be true, because when tragedy hit me and put a hole in my own soul, I was flooded with a flurry of thoughts and questions like that coming at me from all sides. I knew they were from the enemy. He was trying to drive a wedge into my relationship with God and get me to resent Him or hold Him responsible for my pain.

Sin's Role in This Conflict

Before we go any further, I want to explore one statement about all these questions that we must know and believe to stay on track. God's Word backs it up. Romans 5:12 (NKJV) says, "...through one man, sin entered the world, and death through sin..." *All* sin and evil, along with their horrible consequences, are a result of man exercising *his* free will in choosing to operate independently from God's standards and His plan.

There are fully seven different words describing and de-fining "sin" in the Bible, but the most commonly used defi-nition – cited 221 times—is actually an archery term, taken from the Greek word "Hamartia." *Hamartia* means "to miss the mark," as in an archery competition, and therefore fail to receive the prize or blessing. In ancient times, archers did not shoot with modernized gear or at short distances. They shot at very long range, almost like what we today would consider old school artillery. They would rain down arrows on their opponents from castle walls, or from pro-tected areas behind foot soldiers as they advanced. As a result, competitions also involved shooting at great dis-tances. It was called field archery. To facilitate the competi-tion, a spotter would position himself halfway to the target and when an archer hit the target, the spotter would shout "Mark!" When the target was missed, he would let the archer and the judges know by shouting "Sin!" In other words, to "sin" is to miss the mark.

When God created us in His own image, He gave us a free will, just like His. He knew this was risky, because He knew man could choose to operate by his own will rather than God's. Any decision made by man independently from God's will would surely fall short of His plan and pur-pose and intent, causing man to miss the mark.

Right from the start, God told Adam and Eve about this danger. He said that there are two trees in the Garden of Eden—the Tree of Life and the Tree of the Knowledge of Good and Evil. He gave man a choice. Eat of any tree in the Garden, but do not eat of the Tree of the Knowledge of Good and Evil, or you will die. So, right from the start, there have been two choices, two ways to live, and, ultimately, two groups of people in the world. One group would choose to use their free will to live in harmony with their Creator. The other group would choose to sin and miss the mark by using their freedom to do what they wanted and live life their own way. This latter choice has also resulted in the development of false religion and false gods that people have fashioned after their own perception of God, or due to demonic delusion. All in all, history has shown the catastrophic consequences of sin in the universe, along with its consequential downward spiral into eternal judgment and separation from God.

Contrary to the accusation that He is responsible for all of the horrible consequences of man's sin, God is actually the author of all that is good. James 1:17 (NKJV) teaches that "Every good gift and every perfect gift is from above, and comes down from the Father of lights..." By comparison, God makes an interesting statement in the Bible about Satan. He said, "I have created the waster to destroy" (Isaiah 54:16, KJV). In John 10:10 (NKJV), Jesus said this about the contrasting agendas of Satan and Himself with respect to mankind: "The thief (Satan) does not come except to steal, and to kill, and to destroy. I have come that they may have life, and that they may have it more abundantly."

Good Triumphs Over Evil

I would like you to keep a very important thing in mind as we go forward; evil cannot ultimately triumph over good; unrighteousness is not stronger than righteousness. The Cross proved that. At the Cross, Jesus yielded His life to His enemy and let him do his worst. God could have stopped Satan. Jesus Himself said to His disciples that He could have called to His Father and thousands of angels would have come to rescue Him (Matthew 26:53). The Bible says this about the Cross, "The foolishness of God is wiser than men, and the weakness of God is stronger than men" (1 Corinthians 1:25, NKJV.)

The Cross is the pinnacle of the clash between good and evil. At the Cross, good let evil do its worst, and seemingly evil won. The Cross was Jesus, the Son of God, yielding in utter weakness to Satan's attack, and it seemed foolish to let His enemy do this to Him without a struggle, but look at what really happened. The only thing that really happened was that Jesus suffered and paid the penalty for all our sins so we could be freed from Satan's power. The Bible says in Colossians 1:13 (NIV), "For He has rescued us from the dominion of darkness and brought us into the kingdom of the Son He loves." In other words, God let the enemy do his worst to Jesus and as he did, Jesus won freedom from sin, death, and hell for every member of the human race who would believe in Him and accept His free gift.

At this point, I saw something interesting in the story of the cross that parallels Job's story. Satan did his worst to Jesus and God let him do it. However, in the process, Satan lost control of billions of people who would receive God's forgiveness; he lost his position and sealed his doom. The Cross was God at His seemingly weakest point; Jesus took the worst hit possible. God just let Satan do it. But Satan in his strongest, most domineering moment absolutely lost on all sides. 1 Corinthians 2:7-8 (NKJV) says this about the demonic powers of this world: "But we speak the wisdom of God in a mystery, the hidden wisdom which God ordained before the ages for our glory, which none of the rulers of this age knew; for had they known, they would not have crucified the Lord of glory."

So, an interesting point to make here is that righteousness and goodness in their weakest yielded state are infinitely stronger and more powerful than evil in its full strength. First Corinthians 1:18 (NASB) says: "The preaching of the Cross is foolishness to those who are perishing. But to those who believe, it is the power of God."

I have always been intrigued by verses like Joel 3:10, "Let the weak say, I am strong," and 2 Corinthians 12:9: "...my strength is made perfect in weakness." These verses doubly intrigued me at this time and season of my life and circumstance. I was feeling weak, needy, knocked

23

down, and hurting from the blows that tragedy had inflicted. I felt a fellowship with Job in his tragic circumstances. He too, was torn, weak, and sitting in sackcloth and ashes.

Jesus was weak, beaten, and torn as He experienced suffering far worse than anyone else ever had, but He went through it all and in it He triumphed over death, hell, and the grave. He opened a pathway to eternal life for the entire human race. All of these victories came out of His pain and weakness. Through some mysterious, wonderful means, all of these tremendous outcomes were a result of weakness and suffering. I determined that I too, would find strength in my weakness. I felt hope rising in me, knowing that somehow, someway, something wonderful and beautiful could come from my painful, trying circumstances. And, in fact, amazing things did happen, as I will tell you about when we get back to more of my story. But first, let's finish looking at Job.

Job's Response to Personal Tragedy

As I continued to read the book of Job, the next thing I noticed was Job's response and reaction to the tragedy that had struck him. Job clung to God and did not accuse God of any wrongdoing. He knew better. He did not understand all the whys, but he knew God loved him. He knew God was in control and so he worshipped God in his pain. "Then Job arose, tore his robe, and shaved his head; and he fell to the ground and worshiped." (Job 1:20, NKJV) Worship is powerful. It unites us with God's will and purpose in any situation. It also helps us keep our perspective to see beyond our present pain. It is like a zoom lens that allows you to zoom out, and it keeps you from being swallowed by circumstances. Pastor and author Mark Batterson states, "Worship is forgetting what is wrong with you and remembering all that is right about God." It is like hitting the refresh button on your computer.

24

What Job chose to do in his time of heartache resonated with me. I was a worship leader for many years, and during that time I learned the value of worshipping God in every circumstance. I remember thinking that, like Job, I must cling to God no matter what, if I was going to see all things work together for good. I went to band rehearsal just two days after the funeral for my wife and daughter. I played guitar and worshipped in all three services on that following Sunday, and in the Wednesday and Saturday services as well. It was hard, but by God's grace I was able to do it. I just hung onto God and worshipped Him.

During the next period of my life, for a number of months I remember just slugging it out, putting one foot in front of the other, simply doing my best to survive. It felt a lot like what people have described to me about how they feel when they hit burnout. All the zest for life seems to disappear. There seems to be no gas or energy for any movement in any particular direction. That is exactly what I experienced. It was during this period that I relearned the importance of doing what is right, and not necessarily acting and making decisions based on the way we feel. Feelings and emotions are fickle. They are wonderful in the proper realm of human expression, but they certainly are not reliable directives to navigate life's challenges. We are all so different in our makeup, and we all tend to react in so many different ways when we take a hit, or when tragedy touches our lives. One tendency is to shrink back and become withdrawn, even reclusive. That is exactly how I felt for a time. As I look back now, I think it would have been quite harmful if that reclusiveness had continued for very long. Every time I would feel a heaviness pushing me down, I would put on some good praise and worship music and just listen to it and praise God in spite of the way I felt. The Word of God actually prescribes praise as a remedy, describing it as a garment that covers the spirit of heaviness (Isaiah 61:3).

Worshipping God opens your spirit and keeps you from going into a downward spiral. Worshipping is an overt act of yielding and surrendering to God; it's making yourself weak on purpose, putting God's will in your life ahead of anything else you might be feeling or wanting to do. The voice of worship is essentially stating, "God, You are bigger than the situation I am in, and You will carry me through. You can make a way for me where there is no way, and work it all out for good." When we take this approach, God's unseen power brings a divine enablement into our lives that lifts and empowers us to carry on and go the distance. Because this is such an important facet in overcoming the setbacks that we face in life, I will share some more valuable things that I have learned about the incredible power of worship a little later on as well.

Chapter 3 - Don't Get Hijacked

The Cosmic Wager between God and Satan was in *full* swing. Satan had challenged the quality of Job's relationship with God and accused God of blessing Job to get Job to love Him. He had further stated that Job would abandon his relationship with God if God were to stop blessing him. In response, God said "Ok, do your satanic thing; we'll see what the result is." As we have seen, Satan brought a devastating attack on Job's family and his estate, and Job lost everything. As I studied and read Job's story, I felt such an identification with Job and what it must've been like for him at that moment. I took note that Job held firmly to his relationship with God. He never budged. He never developed any wrong mindset about God or accused Him of anything, even though he didn't fully understand what was going on. He tore his clothes (as was the custom in that day) to show his extreme grief and loss. Job emphatically acknowledged God as his source for everything. Even in his grief, he worshipped and thanked God and firmly clung to his faith. I knew I must do the same if I were to see any good come out of everything I was going through.

The first round score: God 1, Job 1, Satan 0. As time goes on, though, another incident occurs in the heavenly realm. In this event, God gives us another rare glimpse into what is going on behind the scenes in the spiritual world. Satan appears before God again, and again God initiates the conversation. I'll let you read it for yourself in Job 2: 1-8.

Job 2 (ESV)
Satan Attacks Job's Health

¹Again there was a day when the sons of God came to present themselves before the Lord, and Satan also came among them to present himself before the Lord. ²And the Lord said to Satan, "From where have you come?" Satan answered the Lord and said, "From going to and fro on the earth, and from walking up and down on it." ³And the Lord said to Satan, "Have you considered my servant Job, that there is none like him on the earth, a blameless and upright man, who fears God and turns away from evil? He still holds fast his integrity, although you incited me against him to destroy him without reason." ⁴Then Satan answered the Lord and said, "Skin for skin! All that a man has he will give for his life. ⁵But stretch out your hand and touch his bone and his flesh, and he will curse you to your face." ⁶And the Lord said to Satan, "Behold, he is in your hand; only spare his life."

⁷So Satan went out from the presence of the Lord and struck Job with loathsome sores from the sole of his foot to the crown of his head. ⁸And he took a piece of broken pottery with which to scrape himself while he sat in the ashes.

Here again we see Satan challenging God regarding the quality of Job's relationship with Him. Satan states that even though Job had stood firm so far, if he were attacked physically, that would be the end. He would throw in the towel, and abandon his relationship with God. Again, God allows Satan to attack Job. He is infected with boils and sores all over his body. He ends up sitting in sackcloth and ashes (an ancient custom of those in mourning). He is scraping his oozing sores with a piece of a broken pottery jar. I remember reading this the day after I lost my wife and daughter, and though I had never suffered loss to that degree, I felt a real affinity and fellowship with the pain and loss he was feeling. I'm sure that many of you reading this book have taken hits, suffered loss, pain and tragedy at some point in your lives. It is during these times that dozens of thoughts and questions tend to flood our minds. It tends to be a dangerous time spiritually, because the enemy of our souls is trying to separate you and me from God and our purpose in this life. He will mix demonic thoughts into your mind, trying to contaminate your thinking. First come all of the questions. "Why would He let this happen to me if He loves and cares for me?" "Why, for that matter, would He not stop the holocaust of death and pain that goes on every day, all around us?" I just witnessed the news of a horrible massacre of school children in another state, along with the murder of parents and teachers. Finally, to end it all, the demented young man committed suicide. In these moments, powerful thoughts and questions flood the minds of even the staunchest of souls. Why would God let that happen? Where is God? Does He care?

Then, in the second wave of thought, come the doubts. "Maybe God isn't as intimately involved with the human race as I believed He was," or "maybe He has abandoned me," or "maybe there's not even a God." I want to tell you emphatically that Satan's chief tactics are:

Number 1 - to inject thoughts into your mind that question God, His character, and the integrity of His dealings with you and with others. The Bible calls these thoughts "fiery darts of the evil one," in Ephesians 6:16.

Number 2 - After injecting the thought, Satan tries to get you to own the thought as if it were yours, make a personal decision concerning that thought, and then act on it.

Almost immediately after the first wave of demonic questions hit us, the second wave of doubt and uncertainty floods our minds. Again, Satan wants you and me to entertain thoughts of doubt as though they were entirely ours, but I tell you they are not. It is the enemy trying to do to you what he did to Job. He wants you to abandon your relationship with God, or if nothing else, he wants to weaken that relationship by creating uncertainty about God's love and goodness, or of God's ability to truly control the affairs of your life—and the world, for that matter.

Satan's final *coup de grâce* is this: after getting you to question God and then doubt God, now he inserts a conclusive decision about these issues into your mind. The thought generally comes like this: "It is very obvious to me that what I had hoped and believed concerning God isn't entirely true, so I'm pulling back. I pray, and I don't see the answer I hoped for. I'm hurting. You could have helped me, but you didn't, so forget you. If that is all you care, then I don't care. If you are not looking out for me anymore than that, I'm going to look after myself." It may not happen to you exactly the way I just stated, but if Satan can get you to adopt a question about God and adopt a doubt about God's integrity and His sovereignty, and finally get you to adopt the negative decision to abandon God or just pull back a little, he will have hijacked your free will and your faith. He will have undermined to a great degree your relationship with God. He did it to Eve in the Garden. He did it to Job's wife, he tried to do it with me, and he wants to do it to you. That is why the Word of God, in 2 Corinthians 10:5, says that we must recognize and arrest the questions and arguments that Satan uses to assault our minds and take those thoughts captive, and not let them bear bad fruit in our life. (A free roaming thought, wandering unaddressed through your mind, particularly a thought injected by Satan, is a potential minefield, especially if it's a question about God's character or His dealings).

The Trap of Offense

Let's return to Job's story and look at the varying results of Satan's attack in the lives of two different people: Job and his wife. First, when Job was physically attacked with sores and boils and was in utter misery, we see his bottom line response; he said, "Even if God kills me, yet I will trust him" (Job 13:15). Scripture further states that in all these situations Job drew no foolish conclusions about God with respect to what was happening. This attitude and this mindset is the right way to navigate anything that hits our lives, no matter how adverse our circumstances are. No matter how hard, no matter how long, no matter how things turn out, we must cling to God and not listen to Satan's lies and adopt them as our own thoughts. **We must be absolutely convinced and know that God is only good.** He is pure love and, as His Word states in Romans 8:28, "...all things work together for good, for those who love God and are called according to His purpose." This is pure truth, spoken by God Himself. It was true for Job, and it is true for you and me. Satan desperately wants to separate us from God. He wants to get us to question God and then develop an offense toward God that makes us pull back or abandon our relationship with God.

Now let's look at the second person who was affected by Satan's attack on Job. Job's wife had suffered through the devastation of Satan's first attack. Her heart had been ripped out. She had lost her kids and most of her wealth. We don't hear anything positive or negative about her in the first round of Satan's attack; however, when the second wave of adversity hit, she'd had enough. She developed a full blown offense toward God. Her advice to Job: "Abandon your relationship with God, curse God and die" (see Job 2:9). Job's response was, "You are being foolish. Shall we accept only good from God and not trouble?" It goes on to say that Job did maintain a proper mindset and attitude and did not sin (see Job 2:10).

I'm sure that when the first wave of adversity struck, many thoughts flooded the mind of Job and his wife. Some of these thoughts were Satan's lies. When tragedy struck me, my mind was reeling with many "Why?" questions. Many of Satan's attacks on the mind start with a question. He never openly states his endgame. He starts with a seemingly harmless question. I mean, what could be wrong with asking why and wanting some answers?

Job's wife fell right into Satan's trap. She first entertained questions about God and His goodness. Secondly, she entertained thoughts of doubt. "Why is God not helping me? Where is God, anyway? Maybe He doesn't care as much as I thought He did." Then a third wave of conclusive thoughts pounded her mind. "Well, if that's all God cares for me, I'm pulling back, I'm outta here." I said it earlier, but it is worth repeating here: some of the conclusive thoughts may have not even been Job's wife's conclusions, but when questions flooded her mind, she adopted them as her own questions. When doubts about God invaded her mind, she adopted those doubts as her own. Lastly, when conclusive thoughts from Satan about how to respond and relate to God in the future invaded her mind, she adopted them as her own and acted on them. She developed a Satanically-inspired offense against God.

The end result was that she pulled back on trusting God any further and encouraged Job to do the same. Job, however, refused to entertain Satan's habit of questioning God and his lies of doubt. He held to his convictions about God and his relationship with God. Job survived Satan's initial onslaughts, and his story continued. After her iconic statement about what Job should do in response to the tragedies he had suffered, we never hear anything more about Job's wife. She disappears from the pages of history. Hopefully, Job talked her out of her foolish decision to abandon God, and she stayed with Him. Yet her only recorded contribution to Bible history is that she caved in to circumstances and Satan's lies and then disappeared, leaving us with yet another lesson of what not to do. Truly, it is disastrous to allow anything to separate us from our Creator. Job's wife had her faith undermined and her relationship with God hijacked by none other than Satan himself and his lies.

Conquering Doubt

Make no mistake about it; everything I am sharing here is very real to me. I know that—except for the grace of God—I could have been hijacked by listening to the enemy's lies when I was down and hurting. When you take a real hit, you become somewhat vulnerable. I believe turning to God's Word (especially my study of Job) for illumination and strength in my time of trouble was key to discerning what the enemy was trying to do to me. He tried to inject the same lies into my mind that I believe he told Job's wife. It was his attempt to cause me to have an offense with God and separate me from His grace. I will never forget when the enemy tried to do that to me, how I had to go to the Word of God and quote scriptures about His goodness and the fact that He was for me in everything, working it all together for His glory and my good. When the enemy's initial tactic didn't work and he couldn't get me to pin the blame for what had happened on God, he reversed tactics and he tried to pin it on me. He said, "*You* are guilty. God is judging you for some lukewarm area of your life. *You* opened the door to this by not being as good of a husband and father as you should be. This is *your* fault." This was yet another tactic and lie from a cruel, wicked adversary to put guilt and condemnation on me, in order to put me under a cloud of defeat. If you are reading this book and you are beginning to realize this is true about you in some areas of your life as well, stay with me and continue reading. Your spiritual lights are being turned back on, and there is tremendous hope for you.

At this point in my life, I have been in the ministry for many years and have seen many heart-wrenching examples of people who have had their faith hijacked. I recently read about a story told by evangelist Rex Humbard. He told the story of a young man who attended a church service and came under heavy conviction to get right with God and leave his sinful life to serve the Lord. When the opportunity to do so was given, he went forward and got down on his knees in front of the altar. It was customary in those days for church members to acknowledge a person's heart change and come forward and kneel with them in support, as the pastor prayed with the person to get right with God. Tragically, the young man's repentant action was left flapping in the breeze, as no one came forward and kneeled with him. No one joined him or prayed with him. He was left alone, without any help or response. The initial moment of conviction turned instead into a moment of rejection, anger, and the pain of being abandoned. The young man got to his feet and left the church, and as he left, he spat out to his sister, Audrey, "That is the last time I will ever darken the door of any church." It was one promise he kept. That tender moment of conviction disappeared and was replaced by a full-blown offense. I can almost hear the quick punch that the enemy inserted in his thought process to do him in. "All these so-called Christians are hypocrites; nobody cares about you, and God doesn't care either. You're on your own, buddy." The young man adopted those lies as his own conclusion about God, and the church. The man's name was John Dillinger. He went on to become a robber and a murderer. Eventually he became public enemy number one, at the very head of the FBI's most wanted list. He died a violent death in a shootout with law enforcement officers. If someone would have come and prayed with him, he might have committed his life to God, and his life story and his eternal destiny would've been greatly different.

As a side note, even though I don't have all the facts and I was not there, I can't help but think that those church members missed a tremendous opportunity to minister grace and salvation. Instead, they ministered rejection. There is, at the very least, one lesson in this story for all followers of Jesus. We must make sure that our words and actions never give the enemy ammunition to create offenses for people who are seeking to find God. Sadly, the road of history is littered with the body bags of those who have been separated from God by adopting Satan's lies into their thought life. Eventually, they shrink back and develop an offense. Then they grow cold and wander away from God. On my way home from church just yesterday, a man texted me and said, "Pastor, I'm so discouraged. My marriage is failing. I think I'm falling out of love with my wife. I'm thinking it's over, and I'm wanting to throw in the towel. I just don't think I can turn things around." I can almost hear him adopting those demonic lies being whispered to him as his own thoughts. Another email I just received said, "Pastor, God isn't answering any of my prayers; I'm wondering why I pray at all." Hmmm!

Along these same lines, yet in a somewhat different vein, I recently sat with a young married man who was struggling for his life against vice and addiction. It was threatening his family, his marriage, and his business. He was totally overwhelmed and depressed to the point of suicide. He had committed his life to Christ sometime before, but he had bought into the demonic lie that now he was too far gone, in too deep; he started believing the lie that he could not overcome his addiction, and that there was no hope for him.

I also remember sitting with Paul and Aleta Penfold, a couple who are dear friends of our family. They had just been devastated by the tragic loss of their son. Paul had found his son, Justin, dead in a basement where he had been painting, overcome by fumes of the lead-based paint. When Paul found him, he carried his son outside and performed CPR, but unfortunately, it was too late. He held his son in his arms and begged God to revive him, but nothing happened. As a result, Paul's emotions were flooded with everything from helplessness to anger, frustration, and anguish. He told me honestly that, for one extreme moment, he felt as though he would have been willing to make a deal with the devil himself to get his son back.

I should mention here that this was the second son that this couple had lost tragically through untimely death. I sat grieving with them and remembered my own pain of having my wife and daughter ripped from me. Then Paul said, "I don't know what to do with how I am feeling. I don't even know how we can we go on. We are devastated, and completely out of gas." So we sat there in a world of unspeakable grief.

You probably want me to tell you what happened next, and what I told them, and how this situation turned out. I will tell you later, but this actually brings me to the central reason I'm writing this book, and to its title and theme. In the next chapter, we will explore some of the aspects of our life's journey and our walk with God that are not always pleasant, and at times can be dark and downright hard and painful. I want to share with you some of the things that I have discovered in my season of pain and trouble, that have brought me to a deeper understanding of God and His ways. The end result of it all was, when I burst into the clear from that dark, painful period of my life, I was *more* free and *more* secure in God's love than I had been before the tragedy. I found that somehow through it all, I had acquired a greater degree of gratitude and appreciation for others, along with a reckless trust in God that has brought me a new, elevated zest for life, along with fresh vision and hope for the future. It is my hope and prayer that as I share with you what I have learned, you will experience the very same thing.

Chapter 4 - Faith's Darker Side

Job 5:7 (NIV) - Yet man is born to trouble as surely as sparks fly upward.

Psalm 71:20-21 (NIV) - Though You have made me see troubles, many and bitter, You will restore my life again; from the depths of the earth You will again bring me up. You will increase my honor and comfort me once more.

So what is "The Dark Side of Faith?" Before I answer that question, I would like to state something very important that we must know and understand. We live in a fallen world, with the results of man's sin and disobedience from the fall. God does not shield us from all the pain and dysfunction of this age; rather, He works within it to build His unseen kingdom in you and through you. He is not the author of all the consequences of sin: pain, death and hardship. Those are the fault of man and the result of sin. But, God uniquely works within this broken framework to build His perfect kingdom in us and through us. With that stated, the Dark Side of Faith is this: **In your walk with God you may experience hard, painful things that have nothing to do with your comfort, your temporary welfare, your contentment, or personal gain.** However, God is using these things as a necessary part of your life's purpose. Number one, they are key to your personal growth and development, and number two, God is using everything in your life's experience to uniquely position you as a vital piece in His grand design. He wants to use you to build His kingdom. To do this, He must shape you; He must mold you, and through every one of life's experiences He is uniquely moving you along, positioning you through every circumstance and each scenario for His grand design.

Ravi Zacharias provides a great example of this whole process in his book, *The Grand Weaver*. He was in Delhi, India and looking at the beautiful saris (traditional garb that many Indian women wear). He looked in one shop window and saw an especially beautiful sari made for a bridal gown. Curious, he decided to step into the shop and see how these beautiful gowns were being made. Essentially, each gown is crafted by a father and son team. The father sits on a raised platform, with huge spools of brilliantly colored threads within his reach. The son sits on the floor facing him in the lotus position. Their fingers move nimbly, their eyes focused on the pattern that is slowly emerging with each move of the shuttle. At first, the pattern is unrecognizable, but gradually, as things progress, a grand design appears. The father gathers some threads in his hand, then nods. The son moves the shuttle back-and-forth. A few more threads, another nod, and again the son responds by moving the shuttle. The process goes on and on with much repetition. Occasionally, curious shoppers step into the shop and ask questions about the whole process. The father pauses his work for the moment and responds politely by trying to explain the picture that he has in his mind, but compared to the magnificence of the final product, the description is very insufficient. Eventually, all of the spools of thread are almost empty and a beautiful, 6-yard long sari gown—breathtaking in its colors and with all of its splendor—has been produced.

Throughout the entire process, the son has had a lot easier task than his father. Most likely, he often was even bored, wishing for some other calling in his life that was more stimulating or fulfilling. He basically has but one task: namely, to move the shuttle as directed by his father's nod, hoping to learn to think like the father, so he can carry on the family business when that time comes. Yet the whole time, from beginning to end, the design has remained in the mind of the father as he held the threads.

If an ordinary weaver can take a collection of colored threads and create a breathtakingly beautiful garment, then how much more can the grand designer of the universe, who created it all out of nothing, make something beautiful out of our lives? Yet to an even greater degree than the son who participated in the weaving of the sari, we must embrace the whole process and learn to think like our Heavenly Father.

Growth is Essential

I think a huge mistake many people make when they come to faith in Christ, is to continue to relate to God as a child over the long term, and not grow up. When I first came to Christ, I was like a child. I couldn't see much farther than my own personal need for the moment. Obviously, I was trying to get my life on track. I was looking to God as the source of blessing and meeting my needs. This is very normal for a child. As time went on, however, it's almost like I began to look at God as the great slot machine in the sky, ever existing to meet my needs and bless me. I heard lots of popular teaching on how you could take God's promises and claim them by faith. Then, just insert a promise into the slot machine in the sky (God), pull the lever (just believe it, confess it, and speak it), and wait for the answer. I wasted no time in stacking up Bible verses like cordwood about promises and blessings regarding all of the things I either wanted or needed. It wasn't long, though, before I became very frustrated. I didn't get many of the things I was claiming from God and believing Him for. I wondered what was wrong. It is very normal to be childish at first, for children are what we are. Children, especially the younger ones, are self-centered, merely self-aware, and needy. They have no concept of a grand design or big picture.

As I consider this concept, I am reminded of one of my younger sons in particular. What a joy he has been! He is the center of his universe. He views me as his source. He thinks I am there at his beck and call, to meet his needs, and that I am orbiting his universe. He thinks I am ever present as his great supplier, and he is horribly disappointed when I don't come through for him. He loves me as his dad—heart and soul, no mistake about that—but he is forever trying to use me to set himself up in his little universe. I, on the other hand, am far more interested in his overall growth and development than his present comfort. I want him to be happy and fulfilled, but many times I must say "No" to him or hold him back. I know what's best for him. I see his future and the big picture; he does not. If I made it all about him in the moment, met his every need, and only addressed his personal, temporal happiness, it would be enabling him to stay in a selfish, immature state and not grow up.

And so it is when we come to Christ. We are like small children. We are needy, self-centered, in need of help. We are looking for salvation, for forgiveness, and for grace. We need Him to help us, and He does. Then we learn about the promises in His word. He tells us to trust Him. He tells us to ask Him for what we need. We learn to look to Him as our father, as our supplier, as the one who answers our prayers; however, we still tend to view our lives and purpose through the lens of our limited perspective.

Going back to my reference to the man who texted me and said, "Pastor I just feel like God is not answering my prayers and I wonder why to even pray anymore," I believe that the right response to that would be that God answers our prayers in a number of ways. First of all, "No" is an answer. "Wait" is an answer. The problem is many times that we have expectations about how we want God to come through for us, and when it doesn't happen that way, we become disappointed and even discouraged. I would like to take the liberty of rephrasing what I heard that man say to me when he texted me about his disappointment concerning the results coming from his prayers. I heard him say, "I had an expectation of what I wanted God to do for me and I prayed and claimed a scripture verse and it hasn't happened." When our preconceived expectations of how God is going to come through for us are dashed, that doesn't mean He is not answering our prayers. We need to reject the enemy's lying thoughts that he would try to insert into our minds to try throw us off course and cause us to become disillusioned with God.

There is no higher example for how to navigate and stay on course with God when the answer is "No" than Jesus. As the time of His crucifixion drew near, He prayed in the garden of Gethsemane and said, "Father, please take this cup of suffering I'm facing away from me...please, if there's any way to avoid it." Jesus was literally sweating blood at the moment, which is indicative of off-the-chart stress levels – body, soul, and spirit under extreme duress. But he tagged the end of His prayer with the doxology that every believer should pray, including the man who texted me. Jesus said, "Nevertheless not my will, but Your will be done." God's answer to Jesus' request at that point, when His son was in the worst position possible, was "No." In effect, He said, "Son, there is a high purpose and plan that I have for you that you must continue to embrace. I cannot meet your expectation or request the way you would like it at this time."

Many times we try to use the promises contained in scripture in the wrong way and claim them out of context or through the lens of our own expectations. This is a mistake. We have a very limited view and perspective of the overall picture. I believe in all the promises in the Word of God. I believe in claiming the blessings in the Word of God. I believe in standing on them. But we must always tag every prayer with, "God, not my will, but Your will be done, in every situation." When we do this, we are submitting our expectations to God and making them secondary to His will and purpose for us, even if it includes "no" or "not yet." Eventually, God wants us to grow up. He wants us to learn to work with Him and learn His ways.

The primary thing we need to keep in mind as we endeavor to grow up is this one very important fact: **it's not about us.** Our lives are not at the center of everything, with God orbiting our universe to meet our needs. Rather, God's Kingdom is the center, and our lives are revolving around the kingdom of God and His purposes. I want to say it again: it's not about us. Our lives stand for something much bigger, something much grander than our own existence, and yes, even our own happiness and well-being.

I heard of a Normandy war story in World War II where hundreds of troops were pinned down on the beach under enemy gunfire. The Commander in charge ordered several of his men to take out an enemy machine gun nest, called a "pillbox." He loved those men. He cared for them. He cared for their welfare. He knew he was sending some of them to certain death. However, because of what was at stake, he was willing to send them into harm's way and maybe even cause them to die for the greater good. As it turned out, several of the men were killed, but one of them managed to get a grenade into the enemy's machine gun nest, thus ending the crisis. Hundreds of Allied lives were spared, and the campaign advanced.

The Bigger Picture

And so it is with our lives; God sees the big picture. He knows the end from the beginning. Our lives are connected to that picture. Sometimes, we are frustrated when our prayers seem unanswered. We are frustrated by events and things that happen which we don't understand. Sometimes, these things are dark, painful, and unpleasant. But, if we could see the big picture, we would see just how wonderfully God positions our lives through every circumstance, and how wisely He handles our prayer requests. Many times the delay that we see in answered prayers is because there is a huge difference between our timing and God's divine timing, related to the big picture. Remember, God is uniquely positioning your life as a vital piece of the big picture—the image of His eternal kingdom—and there are many aspects of overall timing for Him to work out as He fits everything perfectly together. Meanwhile, He is building His character and nature in you and using you for His purposes.

There is yet another potential danger related to our prayers and our expectations as to how God should answer them. If God really answered all our prayer requests quickly and efficiently—the way we would expect Him to—very soon we would be using God to define our universe as we see it, and we would in effect move God into a servile position, supposedly at our beck and call. But that is not the way it is. The Lord 's Prayer states this very clearly: "Your kingdom come, Your will be done on earth as it is in heaven." It's all about God's kingdom, and our lives orbit His kingdom purposes.

God is using everything—even the hard, painful things that we experience—to shape and position our lives for His divine purpose, and as we shall see, we play a key role in building God's kingdom and dismantling what Satan is doing in the earth. It may be difficult for us to grasp, but we need to come to grips with the fact that God is willing to let us suffer pain, discomfort, and even dark things for the greater good of building His kingdom. This is not to say that God is the author of these things, or that He takes any pleasure in seeing our suffering. It's just that in His infinite wisdom, He can find a way to bring something good from even the darkest situations. From our limited perspective, some of these things may seem to make no sense at all, but as we see from Job's life and his story, a lot of times something much greater is going on behind the scenes. From the natural perspective, Job just looked like a man who was in a miserable state. He lost most of his possessions; his children perished in a storm. His life was in shambles, and it looked like it was all bad with no good in sight...no hope, no comfort. Even Job's wife cashed in her chips about God and His goodness. But as we can see, God had a real reason in His eternal purpose in allowing Job to suffer. Through this example, He gave billions of believers throughout history a glimpse into the spiritual realm, allowing them to see what goes on behind the scenes. He let them see what's at stake with their own lives, and gives them an understanding of God's sovereignty and omnipotence and His complete control over the universe, including anything Satan tries to do. It is important to note that Satan couldn't do anything to Job without God's permission. In that light, it might also appear that God was somewhat to blame for Job's pain. But in no way is this true, any more than it would be true of the commander in our earlier story who sent some of his men to certain death. He was not responsible for the war, the pain, and the death and killing going on; however, he orchestrated events in a very critical situation to bring about the best result. The commander was willing to sacrifice his men and expose them to pain and possible death for the greater good, to bring an end to the fighting and bring freedom and justice to many people who were suffering in the bondage of tyranny.

I want to say it again—the dark side of faith is this: it is all the pain, suffering, discomfort and trials you must go through in this life. The primary purpose for this is to shape your character to become Godly. A second purpose God has for you is, He wants to uniquely position your life to accomplish His divine purpose for you. Jesus is our pattern and our example in this regard. 1 Peter 2:21 (NIV) states, "To this you were called, because Christ suffered for you, leaving you an example, that you should follow in His steps." Romans 8:29a (NKJV) says, "For whom He foreknew, He also predestined to be conformed to the image of His son." God allowed Jesus to suffer to promote and build His kingdom for the greater good, which included salvation for all who would receive His grace and believe in Him. God is also willing to let us suffer and endure trials, troubles and discomfort for His glory and for our ultimate good as well. He has extremely lofty plans for us in the future. 2 Timothy 2:12a (KJV) says, "If we suffer, we shall also reign with Him."

Incidentally, this would be a good time to remember something very important that we keep saying: it (life and its events) is not about us…it's not about you and me. But, the brutality of the cross—**the whole extensive redemptive plan spanning thousands of years—*was* all about us.** It was an act of pure, selfless, painful love. God, the divine Parent, gave His only son to pay for our sins. He paid the ultimate price to redeem us and return us to our original purpose. He loved us first. While we were still sinners, Christ died for us. He gave Himself to us first. John 3:16 (NIV) says, "For God so loved the world that He gave His one and only Son, that whoever believes in Him shall not perish but have eternal life." Now, we belong to Him and we are His children. Our divine parent loves us far too much to leave us in the condition in which He found us. He is willing to let you and me suffer and go through many hardships in this life to build His nature in us, conforming us to the image of His son.

Further, He wants to use you and me to build His kingdom and assist in bringing the message of salvation to a lost and dying world. We share in Christ's role and ministry. Romans 8:28 states that, ultimately, all things work together for good to those who love God and are called according to His purpose, but that does not erase the fact that we may go through much hardship, including possibly even a very unhappy ending to our lives. Hopefully, this will not be the case for you or me; however, we must remember that our lives revolve around His kingdom purposes. It is not about us.

You may have noticed I have restated these things several times, back to back, almost sounding redundant. Here is why: Satan's number one tactic is to hammer at us with everything he's got to get us to blame God for circumstances in our life (especially things that we cannot understand). He wants to get us to shrink back and pull back in our zeal and passion toward God and the things of God. When we don't see immediate or obvious answers to prayer or things don't go the way we think they should, the enemy does everything in his power to get us to question God with the big questions: "Where are you? Why won't you answer me? Are you going to help me or not? More importantly, are you going to help me the way I expect you to help me?" It is at this critical point and place that **we must trust God at all costs, no matter what our minds are telling us. No matter what the circumstances.**

I discovered an excellent example of total trust in action when I recently went on vacation in Traverse City, Michigan during their annual Cherry Festival. One of the highlights of the festival is a show put on by the U.S. Navy acrobatics jet team called "The Blue Angels." I was at the airport the day before the show, visiting with the pilots and looking at the jets up close. I commented to one of the pilots on how amazing it was that they could stay in such tight formation, performing crazy acrobatics at speeds of up to 700 mph, (while the wings on the jets actually overlap each other and stay exactly 18 inches apart). The slightest discrepancy in their intended flight path would cause a disaster. I said, "It's amazing that you can use guidance systems at that speed that can lock in with such accuracy without fallout or failure." The pilot's next comment amazed me. He said, "No, we don't use electronics for that. It's all visual." My next question was, "How can you look at where you're going, and look at each other's wings that are only 18 inches apart, overlapping each other at the same time?" He replied, "You can't do that. Only one person looks where we're going. We call him 'the Boss.' He calls the shots. The rest of the team only looks at their wings and the distance between them. We keep our eyes locked on our wings. If the Boss makes a mistake, it would be disastrous. We could all be dead. It demands total faith in your leader, total trust in him, and total obedience to his every command." Shivers raced up and down my spine upon hearing this perfect correlating example of how it is to be with us and our Heavenly Father.

Chapter 5 - Why Does God Delay?

Sometimes, there seems to be a huge delay in the things we would like to see happen in our lives. We pray and ask God for things. We claim promises in the Bible, but sometimes they just don't immediately happen and we feel like we are on disconnect with God. To top everything off, sometimes we experience circumstances and hard times that tempt us to almost wonder if God is aware of us or paying any attention to us, but if we trust Him during those times, **God has a provision of grace** that will sustain you in whatever you are going through. It will move you forward in His will and plan. On top of that, in the future as you look back on those trials, you will see that God had a definite purpose in allowing you to go through those things. God is in complete, total control of our lives. His interest in us and our affairs goes down to the most detailed level of our lives and thoughts. To illustrate this, He said that even every hair on our heads are numbered (see Matthew 10:30). Knowing these facts as you go on in your walk with God is a very important factor in trusting Him during times of trouble and testing. You will find yourself resting in God with peace in your heart and mind, instead of becoming discouraged and frustrated.

There is a story in the Gospel of John, Chapter 11, which perfectly illustrates this point. You may read the account yourself, but I will paraphrase it for you here. The chapter starts off by saying that Lazarus was sick. (Jesus had three dear friends who lived in Bethany, named Mary, Martha and Lazarus). Lazarus became very sick and was dying, and Mary and Martha sent word to Jesus and said, "Please come quickly, so you can pray for him and heal him." What is amazing is that when Jesus got the news, it says He deliberately delayed in coming to pray for Lazarus. He intentionally stayed several more days where He was, instead of going right back to Bethany. He said the reason was for the glory of God. Shortly thereafter, Lazarus—who I'm sure was hoping desperately that Jesus would come along—died and was buried. When Jesus got the news that Lazarus was dead, He then decided, "Okay, now let's go to Bethany."

On the surface, this seems like quite a strange story, seemingly implying that Jesus was uncaring and almost deliberately holding back what He could have provided to His dear friends. When He neared the village, Mary ran out to him crying and said, "Master if you had only been here, my brother would not have died." Then Jesus went to the gravesite with the family and stood there and cried. He felt their pain. He felt their loss. And, because Lazarus was a dear friend, it was His loss as well. But as He stood there, Jesus knew that God had wanted to do something greater with this moment than just heal Lazarus or meet temporary needs, no matter how desperate they were. He realized there was a lid on everyone's faith. They all believed He could have healed Lazarus if he were still alive, but they could not see or believe anything further than that. They could not see God's infinite provision with power over even

death itself and the grave. There was a limit on everyone's faith and their capacity to believe in Jesus. Furthermore, God wanted to use this situation, even though it caused Lazarus and his family great pain, to forever show billions who would read this story in scripture through the ages that He is the resurrection and the life and that He is Lord over death and everything beyond the grave. I believe He also raised Lazarus to give all who believe in Jesus and His Word a living hope of our own resurrection when we die.

The story continues with Jesus praying that everyone who would ever read this story or was involved at the present time would get a greater revelation of who He was. He then called the dead man out of the tomb, by saying "Come out!" By this time, Lazarus had been dead for four days, but he did indeed come out of the tomb, fully alive, though still bound in grave clothes. Jesus said, "Unwrap him and let him go." In this story, is interesting to note a number of very important things. **Sometimes, God delays in meeting our immediate need.** He will not come through for us when or how we expect. But if this happens, there is something greater and more important that He wants to accomplish. Furthermore, during these times of uncertainty, we must hold onto God and His promises more tightly than ever, and not allow ourselves to be separated from Him or pull back from Him, because on the other side of that trial, tragedy, or circumstance lies His provision, His purpose, and the end result of whatever He intended for us. In this situation, Jesus blew the lid off the faith of all who witnessed these events and gave everyone a greater capacity to believe in Him and who He was. He could not only heal people from their ailments and sicknesses, but He had power over death itself, and the capacity to give people eternal life. In addition, He gave everyone who would ever read this story the same revelation, the same hope, and the same understanding. Lastly in this situation, He actually did raise Lazarus from the dead and brought joy and fulfillment to the family. Looking back at this event after the fact, it is certainly easy to see that God had a real purpose in that family's pain and loss, and that the tremendous spiritual lessons conveyed in this story, read and shared throughout the ages by many millions of people, have been more than worth the pain and discomfort it temporarily caused them.

Delay and Perfect Timing

I remember a story from my own life, not too long ago, that parallels all the things we have just shared about why God delays sometimes. I was playing softball with a group of young people at a church picnic. I temporarily forgot that I was no longer a kid and started playing like a madman. I was wearing flip-flops that day and they got in my way, so I kicked them off and played barefoot. I charged around the bases, pounding the ground with my bare feet, and went running through the outfield as well. I did this for probably around an hour to an hour and a half. The next day, the heels of my feet were quite bruised from having had no support during my softball renaissance. Then, over the next couple of weeks, I developed plantar fasciitis (a highly painful foot condition). I tried doing the things I was recommended to do to put it behind me, but it got worse. I began to limp around. It was painful to walk. I began to take a powerful anti-inflammatory every day to be able to walk around without too much pain. I prayed and claimed scripture verses about healing, particularly one of my favorites, Isaiah 53:5 (NIV), that states, "But He was pierced for our transgressions, He was crushed for our iniquities, the punishment that brought us peace was on Him, and by His wounds we are healed."

Healing is one of the provisions and blessings that God provides for us through Christ's sacrificial death for us. Healing is also one of the signs that God uses to show His love and grace to a lost and dying world. Mark 16:18c

(NKJV) states, "They [believers] will lay hands on the sick and they will recover." I have prayed for healing for many people over the years, in crusades, church services, and privately. I have seen a number of them supernaturally healed of different ailments, diseases, and various conditions. At other times, though, I saw no visible results. I used to struggle with this inconsistency, wanting to nail the whole subject of healing down as an absolute and build a foolproof case for receiving it; however, though healing is a provision from Christ's atoning work, it is a bit of a mystery as to how God administers healing and when He delays it or doesn't do it at all. That being said, it is our right and privilege to ask for healing, to pray and believe God for healing either through a natural or supernatural means.

During this trying period of time, I remember getting up every day and starting the day by praying and confessing "...Lord, You took my pains and my sicknesses; Lord, You were beaten for me...by Your stripes I claim my healing." I knew from experience that God could heal me instantaneously, over a long period of time, or if it was His will, never. Meanwhile, that didn't stop me from believing in one of God's names, Jehovah Rapha, which means "the Lord your Physician." I believed I needed to be healthy to do what God called me to do and I claimed my healing every day as I limped around, but nothing changed. During this time, I knew I just needed to trust God and I needed to leave the timing of it all up to Him.

In this particular case, I did not allow myself to become frustrated or disillusioned with God or His promises. Yet, still nothing changed. A whole year went by. I thought, "God, pretty soon you're going to have to heal my liver too, from taking all these anti-inflammatories." I remember limping up in the mountainous regions of Wyoming with my bow and arrows, hunting mule deer with my sons. I remember periods of saying every 10 or 15 minutes, "God, You're my healer." I will tell you something that I think is very important. During that time, I developed a tremendous focus on God as my source. I did a lot of looking to God, a lot of depending on God. I drew closer to God. And, I began to sense that at least part of His will in it all was to strengthen my relationship with Him, and for me to learn to walk and work with Him.

As time went on, after favoring my one leg by limping, I started to get pain in my knee, and then it moved up to my hip as well. I remember thinking, "Good grief! This is getting worse and kind of scary." I'm a very active person and I've never been held down for any real length of time by anything. But I kept praising God and claiming His healing. While I was going through my own physical challenges, I prayed for other people during communion services at our church and in special times of worship, and a number of them were touched by God and healed on the spot—but not me.

After a while, it was almost like I forgot about the condition while I continued to minister to other people. I remember one particular service, though, where we had communion and a great time of worship. That day, we had a visiting evangelist who has a dynamic ministry in India. He's known by everyone around the world as Brother Abraham. By that point, I had known him for 30 years and had supported his ministry most of that period of time. He has a network of several thousand churches in India, and is quite an amazing man. He's appeared on *The 700 Club* with Pat Robertson, and he has planned and hosted crusades reaching up to 1 million people, with special speakers like Reinhard Bonnke and other well-known evangelists. After the worship service, I invited him to get up and pray *en masse* for the congregation for anyone who needed healing. I was standing in the front row as everyone stood, and he prayed over the whole audience in general, for God to touch various people who had raised their hands for healing. I did not raise my hand for healing; I was busy praying for everyone else to be healed and not even thinking about my condition. I had basically learned to ignore it, especially on Sundays, when I typically took a maximum dose of over the counter pain reliever so that I wouldn't limp around on stage. While Abraham was praying, though, something very strange happened, something that was not normal. I felt a wind blowing on my face. At first, I thought the air-conditioners (or something) had kicked on and were responsible for the blowing, but there was no air conditioner on. I remember thinking "Wow, what was that?" Meanwhile, we just continued praying for people and went on with the service.

Later that day, when I got home and changed clothes, I suddenly noticed that I felt absolutely no pain or aching in my foot, or my knee, or my hip. Usually, by around 1 o'clock, all the pain meds would wear off and everything would start to hurt again from all the activity. But there was zero pain. In fact, it felt awesome! Suddenly, I remembered the wind and a thought crossed my mind: "Could it be that God healed me at that moment?" I stomped my foot down a little, something I simply could not do without a significant amount of pain. No pain. I slammed my foot down. No pain *anywhere*. I then realized that I had been completely, miraculously healed. I want you to know I am not a flaky person who believes in all kinds of weird phenomenon, nor do I look for or try to embrace those things. I had never experienced anything quite this way before, though, and I didn't argue with it. I was thrilled and actually jumped up and down for joy like a little kid.

It is now several years since that happened, and I have never—ever—had any problem with that foot again. As I look back on that experience, I see in my back trail the tremendous wisdom of God in how He dealt with me through the whole ordeal. When He delayed healing me instantaneously, He really got my attention and I began to look to Him and rely on Him in a greater way. Further, being in this condition helped me identify with people who are suffering and going through trials; I developed a greater compassion for them. Another benefit is that I think the whole experience brought me down a notch and I became a little more humble and a little more God-reliant. It also made me value my health and what a blessing that is. I determined to take better care of myself in the future, because when this body wears out, you're done. Lastly, God's timing and method for healing me was amazing. At the very time this all happened, for a period of several weeks to a month, I had been thinking about cutting back on our church's mission support for Brother Abraham's work in the nation of India. I don't want anyone to think I was being selfish. It's just that Abraham was one of the top three ministries that we were supporting quite heavily, and I was thinking of making a bit of an adjustment and expanding into other areas. My thinking was that we had perhaps peaked in what we were putting into that ministry. I was on the verge of taking action in that regard, and then Abraham came. He prayed. I was supernaturally healed by a wind that came off the platform while he was praying. The message to me was loud and clear: "Doug, you and your church are connected to this man and his ministry. Do not pull back his support."

The reason I share all of this with you is to show you that God has a plan and a strategy in everything that He does that is much greater than ours. He orchestrates everything to keep His will and purpose on course.

Amazingly enough, just one year later, a tremendous revival broke out in one of the provinces in India where Abraham has several churches. As his pastors in that area prayed for the sick people and preached the gospel, miraculous things began to happen and thousands of people began to come from great distances so they too could experience God's presence and hear the Word of God preached. Our church ended up providing a major amount of the financing for a large structure especially built to hold the meetings and shield people from the elements. At this time, we also are at the final stages of raising all the money needed to build a new Bible college in another province. Who could know it? Only the eternal God, who sees the end from the beginning. If He says "No" to you, or He delays and says "Wait," there's a good reason for it. **Have faith.** Trust Him. Hold the line, and what you cannot see will become visible. You may not even be able to fully view the whole picture until you see it in your back trail sometime farther down the road.

I will close this chapter with a powerful lyric from a song called "Sight Unseen," authored by Bob Hartman, and based on Hebrews 11:6:

Sight Unseen

For so long I was depending upon
My senses and fences I tried to ride on.
And trusting in things that can never be seen,
Was always a crutch on which others must lean.
Thinking if I could see I would believe,
Then somebody said believe and you will see
Sight unseen, sight unseen
You have to take it sight unseen.
Sight unseen, sight unseen,
You have to take it sight unseen.
Blinded by the darkness only faith can come between,
Sight unseen, sight unseen.
(Reprinted by permission, Hal Leonard Corp.)

You do have to take it sight unseen...trust God no matter what, and leave the results to Him, no matter what. His will be done in your life.

Chapter 6 - A New Chapter

For the majority of my life, I felt God calling me to the ministry. I had prayed and planned and served God with all my might for many years. All of my plans were to go into the ministry. When I went to Bible college, I married the Assistant Dean of Women, who was also preparing for ministry work. My whole life was poised for ministry. This was my focus. This was my desire, and yet for an extended period of time I could not seem to find clear sailing to get into the ministry full-time as a pastor. God kept putting things in my way that seemed to steer me away from my calling. I kept coming to grips with these different things, though, and finally began to see the wisdom of God in it all. I was determined to learn life's lessons in whatever vein I was in, knowing that He probably had a purpose for it that I simply could not see at the time. Eventually, as I grew and progressed in my walk with the Lord, I came to the point where I thought, "Now I am getting very close to being able to plant a church, preach and teach, and do all the things in my heart I have felt that I should do."

Right when I seemed to be getting there, the love of my life and my youngest daughter were both killed. This tragedy struck a blow that practically took me off my feet. It pulled the carpet right out from underneath me and left me hurting and empty, with my compass needle spinning in every direction. All I could do was hold onto God and His promises. All pursuits of full-time ministry and any other plans I had were completely derailed. I felt myself again journeying away from ministry and the things that were in my heart. I had now been struck a blow in my soul with the things that were dearest to me. During this period of time (that went on for over a year) I clung to stories in the Bible of Joseph who hung onto his dreams even though he went through great hardship. I clung to stories of Job, who lost his loved ones and his possessions. As I said earlier, the one thing I did was to hang onto God's promises and my dreams and the loved ones I had left here. I knew that God works all things together for good for those who love Him. I worshiped God in church and in my quiet times, praising Him, stating that He was in control. I confessed verses in Scripture about the goodness of God. I memorized scriptures like Psalm 23 and quoted verses of comfort, faith, and reassurance ("...even though I walk through the valley of the shadow of death, I will fear no evil, for You are with me)." Even though I temporarily lost my momentum, God gave me the grace to ignore the lies of the enemy, who tried to separate me from trusting in God through doubt, grief, and discouragement.

A Turning Point

After about nine months of battling my circumstances and challenges, (just putting one foot in front of the other and trying to survive), something wonderful and amazing happened to me. I was driving down the road in my old convertible with the top down. The sun was shining. It was a beautiful, crisp, early summer day and I was blasting away the music from some contemporary Christian band and singing and worshiping God along with them. I probably looked kind of foolish to anyone who might be observing or driving by me in another lane. Then it happened, just like that. The cloud of gloom and pain that I had been living under just lifted. I felt a surge of joy. I felt a blanket of peace. I felt the excitement of a new adventure and for what lay ahead of me. In my spirit, I heard the scripture verse, "...My mercies are new every morning." I knew deep in my heart that my wife and my daughter were safe within the everlasting arms. I knew if they were given a chance to come back, neither one of them would have. The Bible states that the joys and pleasures of eternal life far exceed anything in our sphere. I had let them go before, at the grave site, but now I let them go again, on a deeper, spiritual level. The next thing I felt was fresh vision, excitement about the future, and a passion to re-engage with all my might in my life's pursuits, ministry, and anything I might encounter.

I finally admitted to myself that I was no longer married and I willfully entered the world of being a Christian single with kids. Up to now, I had avoided engaging with people who were single. I had tried to act like a married person with all my married friends, but it was very clumsy and strange. But, I finally came to grips with the fact that I was single and there was nothing wrong with being single. The story of this period of my life is probably worthy of a book in itself, but I will keep moving here. I remember the very first time, one night after a church meeting, that I ever went out with a group of singles. I had played guitar in the worship band and afterwards they all asked me to go out for supper. They had asked me before, and I had said "No," refusing to go in that direction. But that night I said, "Yes."

What is very crazy is the fact that on that very first night out, when my resistance had finally crumbled, I met a very interesting lady. She had recently left her church and started coming to our church for a deeper experience in worship and in her walk with God in general. Her name was Caryn. Though we hadn't really met before, she was in the church choir and I was in the band. After this first meeting, though, we began bumping into each other from time to time.

During this same period of time, a number of other very unusual things began to happen as well. I ended up brokering and selling my employer's music business that I had been managing for almost 20 years. I became involved in world missions very heavily, including helping to put together a couple of crusades in India. I put together the ministry team, the financing, and took care of the music and worship as well. Caryn was also involved in these endeavors, as a number of the people from our church participated in the crusade. She headed up the prayer team. I think it was at this point that I begin to take serious note of her commitment to God and kingdom things, related to prayer and godliness. I did not know where it all might be going, but it certainly perked up my attention when I saw these qualities in her. I also found out that she was a physician's assistant and had never been married, and that she very much had her act together on all fronts.

Over the next few months, we found ourselves working together on a number of issues related to overseas ministry. And finally, after many weeks of preparation, our team embarked on our first mission trip to India. We moved from place to place, ministering in a number of areas for three weeks, with the team setting things up for a large regional crusade in the future. We stayed in an old convent in the mountains, where we were protected by armed guards most of the time, because of the great degree of political unrest in the area. Each night after supper, all the couples went to their rooms, leaving me and Caryn by ourselves, sitting and talking in the dining area. At this point, we were the only single people on the trip, so it just naturally seemed to work out that way. After a couple of nights went by, it occurred to me that I was thoroughly enjoying myself and my time with Caryn. I had been married for many years and was in the habit of minding my own business. So this new attraction produced kind of a crazy feeling. I almost felt like I was doing something wrong. To top it all off, the electricity kept going out in the general area that included our facility, so a little Indian boy came in almost every night with a candle for us and we sat talking by candlelight. By the third night, a thought was going through my mind. "God, I really like this lady. Could it be that while I am out here serving You, trying to build Your kingdom, that You are setting me up?"

As time went on, both Caryn and I had a growing realization that God was indeed setting us up for each other, and it turned into quite a whirlwind romance with almost a storybook plot line. At the risk of appearing self-indulgent, I can't help but share one thing that happened that was so unique that when I learned the full details about it later, I realized absolutely that God had truly set me up with Caryn.

Before all of what I just shared happened, on the night before we were to go into a highly regulated area of India, a young man on our team knocked on my door. I invited him in, and he said, "Doug, I need to talk to you about something." I said, "Go ahead." He continued on to say, "Doug, I am in love with Caryn. I can't stop thinking about her. One of the reasons I came on this trip was to be near her. I want to serve and minister to people, but she is one of the reasons why I came. I want to know if you think it's a good thing for me to tell her how I feel. I want to tell her...what do you think?" I immediately instructed him, "Don't even think about it! That will mess up the chemistry of our whole team. We are here to minister to people in a foreign land.

Put your feelings on the back burner, and later on maybe you can talk to her about it, when we get home."

I want you to know I had no personal motive in this, because I was not yet personally interested in Caryn for myself. I simply did what was right. The young man, however, completely ignored my advice. He went from my room straight to Caryn's room and poured out his heart to her, making things a bit awkward, since she did not have the same feelings for him. The next morning, we went into a highly restricted area. All of us were allowed to enter except this young man. When he had his papers checked, they were found to be out of order. He was arrested and taken away under guard. Later, the Christian underground rescued him from the house where he was being kept and smuggled him out of the country, by hiding him under a bunch of rugs on the floor of a taxicab. In a very different fashion, he arrived at the airport along with the rest of us after our three-week stay in the country, thin and pale from his ordeal. To this day, I am not certain what the issue was with his paperwork, or even if there really was anything out of order. Yet, looking back on the whole thing, I realized God had in fact selected Caryn for me and He ejected any and all competition from the picture, from those who may have wanted to pursue her in years past to those who knew her during the time that we became acquainted. In this case, I certainly would have allowed that young man his time with Caryn and would have simply gone to my room and minded my own business, but that's not what God had in mind. I am continually amazed by His personal involvement in every aspect of our lives, on a day-to-day basis. Incidentally, the young man who went through that ordeal recovered quite well and moved on with his life. Soon after that, he met a beautiful young lady from our church, they were happily married, and now he has a wonderful family of his own. God really did work everything out for good for all of the parties concerned.

Some months later, our team undertook a second crusade to India. We engaged in an intense time of ministry for about two weeks. When this episode was over, we were exhausted, yet we were only halfway through our trip. At this point, I remember sitting with Caryn on the third floor of an old hotel where our team was staying. She had tears running down her face and she said to me, "I am so exhausted, I don't know how I can even finish this trip." Right at that moment I knew it was the right time, and I got down on my knees and proposed to Caryn. I presented her with a diamond ring that I had smuggled through customs on my person. (I also threatened to hurl myself off the third-floor balcony if she said "No.") Thankfully, she said "Yes." Six months later we were married, approximately two years after I had lost my wife and daughter. It was a beautiful new beginning to a whole new phase of life.

Setting Priorities

I would like to give some advice here to those who are looking for a mate or have lost a loved one and are considering remarriage. Again, probably a whole book could be written on this to cover the subject properly. But the one piece of advice that I would give anyone would be this: **do not make getting married or remarried your goal, even if it is a deep desire of your heart.** Instead, change your focus and make your main goal pursuing God's will for your life. Also, pursue Christian service in your local church. Hang around with great company, worship God, read the Bible. Stay close to Him and stay strong. Pursue Christian service and God's will with all your might. Run the race as hard as you can, and then, as one minister put it, look to your right and look to your left and see who is running alongside you. That is the kind of quality person you want to be married to. When you are walking in God's will and following His path for your life, you are bound to bump into every good thing He has planned for you.

I remember a prayer I prayed approximately a year after I lost my wife and daughter. It was the same prayer that I had prayed in my early twenties. I asked God to help me in selecting my future wife. I vividly recall what happened a little later, on a beautiful moonlit evening as I was riding down a lonely country road on my Harley. The moon was shining so beautifully and brightly that I I foolishly turned off my headlights. I was riding down the road by the light of the moon, having a real God moment (I'm a bit of a romantic). I heard the Holy Spirit speak to me very clearly. He said to "Go to Christ for the Nations Institute in Dallas. I have a wife for you there. And take your friend, Duane Vander Klok, with you. I have a call on his life for the ministry." Now, many years later, as I recalled this moment, I meditated on the fact that every last thing God had told me to do and had promised me, had happened. My friend Duane became a missionary and Bible teacher in Mexico, and then God led him back to West Michigan where he, along with his wife, Jeanie, built a huge, dynamic, local church with thousands of people in attendance each week. That local church has actually turned into an association of churches across a number of states and countries. And, as I mentioned earlier, I met and married the assistant dean of women of Christ for the Nations Institute. So I prayed again and I said, "God, if you want me to remarry, please pick my companion for me like you did the first time." And that is exactly what happened. Caryn was a perfect match for me and the next phase of my life, even though I didn't realize it fully until later.

Once again, things began to happen like crazy. I got some new business opportunities, and suddenly—after about a year of honeymooning and going through one exciting change after another—Caryn and I sat one morning in church and just looked at each other. At the same moment, we instantly knew we were done with our current phase of serving in our church. We were to be completely done with that part of our life and we were being released for something new. Shortly after that, we felt God leading us to plant a new church in Rockford, Michigan. We started by holding church services in a small school cafeteria, with 35 people attending, and the blessing from the head of our church association - who was none other than Pastor Duane Vander Klok, my friend and roommate from Bible college.

Though it began on a fairly small scale, the church grew very quickly. God enabled us to put together an amazing ministry team. He sent us just the right people. Souls began coming to Christ on a weekly basis. After a few short years, we were able to purchase a good-sized church building and property that had fallen on hard times. Today, as I write this, reflecting back on our whirlwind journey of a little over a decade, I'm amazed at how God has blessed us. We'd just celebrated Resurrection Sunday and had well over 3,000 people at our services. On a weekly basis, we have police directing traffic at all three of our Sunday services to avoid traffic jams on the main boulevard in front of our church. We have a missionary support program that stretches across the country and the world, reaching out to the needy and those who are lost and hurting. And, I have seven wonderful pastors on staff serving in their various capacities. On top of all of this, we are in the middle of a major expansion program to add 30% more room in every area, from the sanctuary to children's ministry to the parking lot.

I have shared all of these things with you to say this: Romans 8:28 (NKJ) says, "All things work together for good to those who love God and are called according to His purpose." We must hold on to God. Hold onto our dreams and believe in His will for our lives in the dark times, in the hard times, in the trying and painful times. If we have made mistakes, causing us and others pain and difficulty, we must ask Him to forgive us and still hang on to

His grace and forgiveness. He is way ahead of all our mistakes and our failures, and knows how to even take those and use them for good, once we get straightened out and get on track.

A Prodigal Comes Home

In addition to my own experience, another prime example of what I have just shared with you can be seen in what happened with my daughter, Carly. I mentioned earlier in the book about how she fell away from God and got angry with God and herself. She tried to inflict pain on herself to lessen the deep pain she was feeling in her soul. Over a period of several years, she dabbled in about everything you could think of: horrible, demonic music; she experimented with drugs, alcohol, the occult, séances, and even some cutting. One night she lay on the floor of her apartment, curled up in a knot. Out of her mind, burned out, ashamed, too afraid to even take her own life, she cried out to God. "God, if You are still there, if You still love me, please take me back as your daughter." She told me later that when she prayed that prayer, instant peace came into her soul. God's presence flooded the room. She came into her right mind and she began to thank God and worship Him right there on the floor. After that, she left her old life; she left the town she was living in, left her friends, and moved in with me and Caryn. She kicked drugs and alcohol cold turkey, and went into missionary training. She became a missionary and ended up becoming a field rep and a response team leader for the para-church ministry, One Hope International.

I remember one very special moment I had with the founder and the president of that amazing ministry, Bob Hoskins. Bob also had a prodigal son named David who had wandered far from the Lord. Through an amazing set of circumstances, he came back to the Lord and was restored. I was at the One Hope International conference and personally witnessed David's humble testimony of gratitude and thanks for his father's and mother's prayers. He then proceeded to symbolically wash his father's feet. On that very same night, many thousands of miles away, my daughter Carly and her ministry team also where symbolically washing the feet of the Romanian national team they had been training to reach their country for the Lord. The two of us have never forgotten that unique, special restorative moment of two prodigals who had strayed so very far from grace. Carly has now been to 25 countries as a missionary and has led many people to Christ.

I remember a particular instance when I was with Carly and we were doing an outreach in a women's prison in Poland. Carly spoke and shared her story, and every lady in the prison meeting but one raised their hands to commit their lives to Christ. She gave them such hope for their lives that they were grabbing onto her and didn't want her to leave. After five years of missionary service, Carly met her awesome husband, who was also working in the field as a missionary. They are happily married and continue to do God's work in a number of different areas as He leads them.

We must never abandon our faith due to guilt or past failures. God can give you a brand new start. He can give our loved ones and those who we are praying for a brand new start. That's just one of the things that is so amazing about grace. Jesus' disciple Peter denied Him three times publicly and cursed and swore to that effect. Jesus forgave him, and he went on to have a world-impacting, dynamic ministry. God's mercies *are* new every morning. Every day is a chance for a brand new start, if we will embrace His promises and His grace and obey the directives He gives us in His word.

As I look back over my life before I became a pastor, I see that everything that I went through—especially the hard times and dark times—were key ingredients to the fruitfulness we are having in ministry now. In the business world for many years, where at times I felt I was being side-tracked and not following my call to ministry, I learned how to manage a business. I learned people skills and how to handle difficult situations and manage money. In volunteer ministry, working without thanks for many years, I learned how to have the right motive and attitude that was necessary for serving on a team. During those times, I vowed that whatever team I put together would not suffer mis-treatment or be taken for granted, but they would be val-ued—every last one of them. During times of death, loss and pain, I learned how to navigate those difficult times without losing my focus, and was given the first-hand knowledge of how to teach others and comfort them, and lead them in their challenging times. Lastly, God perfectly matched and equipped me with my awesome wife Caryn. Her skillset and her abilities are exactly what has been needed for this next phase of life.

Through it all, I have realized on a whole new level that God is always moving us, always maturing and refining us. He is always positioning us, through every circumstance, every trial and every situation, to be exactly where we need to be to bear fruit and do His will. Truly, all things work to-gether for good to those who love God and are called ac-cording to His purpose.

In keeping with this theme, I love Edith Lillian Young's fantastic poem called, "Disappointment, His Appointment."

Disappointment—His Appointment
Change one letter, then I see
That the thwarting of my purpose
Is God's better choice for me.
His appointment must be blessing,
Tho' it may come in disguise,
For the end from the beginning
Open to His wisdom lies.

"Disappointment—His Appointment"
Whose? The Lord, who loves me best,
Understands and knows me fully,
Who my faith and love would test;
For, like a loving earthly parent,
He rejoices when He knows
That His child accepts, UNQUESTIONED,
All that from His wisdom flows.
Disappointment, His appointment
No good thing will He withhold
From denials oft we gather treasures of His love untold.
For He knows each broken purpose
Leads to fully deeper trust,
And the end of all His dealings
Proves our God is wise and just.
Disappointment, His appointment
Lord I take it then as such.
Like the clay in hands of potter,
Yielding wholly to Your touch.
All my life's plan is Your molding,
Let not one single choice be mine.
Let me answer un-repining, Father, not my will but
   Thine.

Chapter 7 - Amazing, Divine Timing

There is a very interesting, comforting scripture that I love and which has helped me navigate many difficult and trying times. It simply states one key fact we must all know, embrace, and rest in. Psalm 31:15 (NIV) says, "My times are in Your hands." Sometimes, when we go through trouble or testing—or periods of life that we don't understand—it is very comforting to know and rest in the fact that God is the master over time and is in complete control over our personal time on this earth. Psalm 139:16 says that His eyes saw our unformed bodies and that all the days ordained for us were written in His book before one of them ever came to be. To me, that's a verse that needs to be meditated on. It is truly a "wow" verse and a "wow" concept. I stated before that the Word of God says every hair of your head is numbered. The Bible says we are His workmanship created for good works. It further states that path of good works for us to walk in was predetermined before we were ever born (see Ephesians 2:10). Another huge point is that God is even way ahead of all our sinful failures and the mistakes that we have made. As we ask forgiveness and get right with God, He will even make those things work out for good in His plan.

The story of Joseph in the Old Testament perfectly illustrates this truth. Joseph was the favorite son of Jacob, the third patriarch in the Old Testament. His father showed him special attention and did special favors for him. On top of this, Joseph was a dreamer and some of his dreams were God dreams about his life and his future. They depicted him in quite a high position. One particular dream showed the sun, the moon, and the stars bowing down to him. Joseph was young, and he somewhat foolishly shared all these things with his brothers. Joseph's brothers became angry and jealous because of all the special treatment he received from their father, along with his self-proclaimed dreams and predictions of them becoming subservient to him. When the opportunity came, they betrayed him, threw him in a pit, and sold their brother to slave traders. Then they told their father that a wild animal had killed Joseph. But, in spite of all the evil and bad things that happened to Joseph, God was way ahead of everyone in His divine plan.

In the natural realm, it seemed like God had completely abandoned Joseph as he went from one bad situation to another. After being betrayed by his brothers, he was sold as a slave to an Egyptian household. But it's interesting to note that God blessed Joseph in that position and he became the head of all the servants and the affairs of that household. After that, when his master's wife tempted him to have an affair, he refused. The woman became angry at being rejected by a slave and lied about him, and his master threw him in prison. There again, God did not deliver him from prison at the moment, but instead blessed him in his situation, and he became the head over all the prisoners. While he was in prison, Joseph got a unique opportunity to speak to two of the pharaoh's personal attendants in regard to their future and destiny. He asked them to remember him and his situation when they came back into favor with Pharaoh. The two men were released from prison just a little later and everything Joseph had ministered and predicted happened to them; one of the attendants was returned to his previous position as the king's cupbearer. The other attendant was condemned and executed just as Joseph had predicted; however, the king's cupbearer—the one who survived—forgot all about Joseph.

I want you to see a pattern in the picture of Joseph's life story. It is absolutely amazing. We see the favored son betrayed, sold into slavery. Then, when he did well, instead of being rewarded he was thrown into prison. In prison, you might think someone could go no lower, but he was forgotten there as well. But, in Joseph's entire downward journey, God was with him and blessed him. God had a purpose in it all. He orchestrated everything to set Joseph up to learn the ways of Egypt and position him to become the savior of the known world during a seven-year period of famine.

Pain and Testing

Here again is another example of God's willingness to let us experience pain and discomfort in this life. He does not wish it upon us. He is not a sadist, but for His purpose and His glory—and our good as well—He will let us suffer in order to test us with the purpose of developing Godly character that will hold up in any situation.

I remember a time in my younger life when I was full of passion, with a driving determination to build God's kingdom with every ounce of strength and energy I had. When it came to a time of possible promotion and recognition, I was misunderstood and denied what I thought was God's obvious next step for me. I was very frustrated. I knew my heart and my motives were sincere. I went home one afternoon all torn up inside and just flipped my Bible open and said, "God please give me something from Your Word." This is not the disorganized form of Bible study and searching for divine direction that I would typically recommend. However, on this day, God spoke to me directly from His Word regarding the story of Joseph and my situation. I have never forgotten it.

This is what it said in Psalm 105:16-22 (NKJV):

^{16}Moreover He called for a famine in the land;
He destroyed all the provision of bread.
^{17}He sent a man before them—
Joseph—*who* was sold as a slave.
^{18}They hurt his feet with fetters,
He was laid in irons.
^{19}Until the time that his word came to pass,
The word of the LORD tested him.
^{20}The king sent and released him,
The ruler of the people let him go free.
^{21}He made him lord of his house,
And ruler of all his possessions,
^{22}To bind his princes at his pleasure,
And teach his elders wisdom.

As I read this, I realized that it was God restricting me and holding me back, not just the people I was frustrated with. I also realized God was testing me and that there must be a reason. I decided not to be offended with God or any person. I decided to embrace and learn any life lessons He had for me at that time. I gave my future to Him, and just worked at being faithful where God had caused me to be for the moment. For a little while, it was one of the more painful, uncomfortable periods in my journey of faith. Many years later, I looked back on that experience and timeframe in my life and I realized that I did not yet have the character that was necessary to do what I am now doing. I had lots of passion and ministry ability, but my character was not up to the same level. Now, I thank God for that time of discipline and His holding me back and testing me. Divine discipline and adjustment are necessary for people who want to do great things for God. It's just flat out not enjoyable, but in the end it yields Godly character and life-bearing fruit. Hebrews 12:11 (NIV) says, "No discipline seems pleasant at the time, but painful. Later on, however, it produces a harvest of righteousness and peace for those who have been trained by it."

It is important that we recognize and embrace these disciplinary periods of our lives and we don't blame the devil for everything. Sometimes it is God who is at work creating circumstances and situations to both test and discipline us. When we learn the life lessons that He brings our way, that season comes to an end, and we move into the next phase of His plan for us. We can see this pattern very clearly in Joseph's story.

In one key moment, Joseph was remembered, taken from the prison, and promoted to the second highest position in the land—second only to Pharaoh himself. Later, when he revealed himself to his brothers, they apologized to him and begged for his forgiveness. He said, "You intended to harm me, but God intended it for good..." (Genesis 50:20, NIV). I want you to notice that God did not shield Joseph from all the evil, pain, and the tragedy of betrayal, hatred, and revenge. Rather, God worked within this whole tragic story to orchestrate His perfect will for Joseph, his family, and the world—this world. **Don't let the enemy lie to you in your mind** and convince you that you have blown it so badly that you have missed your opportunity to serve God and fulfill His purpose for your life. God knew everything that was going to happen in your life long before this present time, and He has even positioned that to work out for His Kingdom and our good, provided that we embrace His grace and return to walking with Him and serving Him.

He's Waiting for You

I love the way God is pictured as a loving, benevolent father in the parable of the prodigal son. It is a story about a foolish young man who asked for his inheritance early, before it was due to him. Upon receiving that inheritance, he went and squandered it in riotous, foolish living. He ended up broke and poverty struck, feeding pigs for a farmer during a time of famine. Meanwhile, the heartbroken father sat on the porch, longing and waiting with open arms for the son to return to his grace and his comfort. When the son eventually came to his senses, he was sorry for what he had done and he went back to his father. When his dad saw him coming in the distance, he ran off the porch to meet him. He hugged him; he forgave him; he restored him back to his original place in the family estate. This is a beautiful picture of God's attitude towards anyone who is sorry for their sins and wants forgiveness. He wants to have a loving, father-son relationship with us. Once that relationship is in place, we can trust Him with our lives and future.

The Bible portrays God as the omnipresent creator and master of the universe. To put this in some sort of perspective, He knows every star by name. He calls them out. He holds them in their place. Every morning the sun rises, and every evening it sets exactly on time. Nothing is ever early, nothing is ever late; the times, the seasons, the galaxies are all held in place by His creative power. Certainly God is able to help us navigate our circumstances and make a way for us. I have seen this in my own life, through various times and seasons. The Bible states in Ecclesiastes Chapter 3 that for everything there is a time and a season. A time to be born and a time to die. A time for planting and a time for harvest. A time to mourn and a time to dance. A time to tear down and a time to mend. A time to be silent and a time to speak. I have been through many seasons of the soul, and as I write this, I am reflecting on one particular season where God made me acutely aware of His intimate and personal involvement with our lives and His profound interest in our daily affairs.

God, the *Real* Estate Agent

As I stated earlier, my wife and I had been called to plant a church in another town. Once we engaged in doing so, we put our home in Byron Center, Michigan up for sale. I knew we would have to move to the city we were working in to be truly involved and effective, not to speak of travel time and convenience. We also began looking for a church building, and we began to look for a new home in the city of Rockford, Michigan. I knew it was God's will for us to move. I knew it was God's will for us to have a church building. So, I was full of expectation and excitement about how He was going to move. But our house did not sell. We could not move on another house. Our hands were tied. The right church building and location were not available either. I had no peace about building a church, though, because we were a new church plant. Building programs are hard, even for strong existing churches. I had no desire to put this kind of burden on a young, growing church.

Despite my original optimism, a whole year went by with no progress on either of these two fronts. I thought, "Wow, this is a big inconvenience, driving multiple hours almost every day." Between my wife and me, we put an astronomical number of miles on our SUV and car. Then, a second year went by. I thought, "Good grief! This is getting old." Then, a third year went by. By now, we were flat out tired. I knew about God's perfect timing; I was tempted to grumble, but I did not. After two years in the real estate market, I had finally pulled my house off of the general market. I slapped a black-and-white "For Sale" sign in the front yard and stopped trying to sell the house in any other way. I admit I became a bit fatalistic at this point and said "Whatever is, will be...God is in control." And, as the theme song of the Disney movie "Frozen" says, I let it go.

Shortly after this period of time, we found a beautiful new parade home in Rockford, Michigan, that had not sold for a year because the housing market had crashed. The sellers had stripped the price down to the bare bones. No sooner had we discovered this home, than a fairly good-sized church building right in our neighborhood, off the same road as the house was on, fell on some hard times and went up for sale. And no sooner did this happen, than someone drove by our home in Byron Center, fell in love with it at first sight, and offered to buy it right off the bat. We went from being on a long, flat line of nothing to a wild melee of craziness. So, shortly after these several discoveries and incidents, we had a miracle week that left me weak. We closed on our old home, we closed on our new home, and we closed on the new church building—all in one week. On top of this, because the housing market had crashed, we bought our new house many thousands of dollars below its original price. Meanwhile, because I had sold my old house for the asking price and without a Realtor, I realized most of what I would've typically lost due to the down market. The purchase price and arrangement for financing on our new church was a miracle. And, on the very first week of our grand opening, we almost doubled in size of attendance. Because of God's unique timing, we prospered in every sense of the word. We need to be patient and let God work. His divine timing is not always the same as our timeframe. During these times of disparity, we must be patient.

As we waited for God's timing to come to fruition, I remember memorizing a number of scriptures and meditating on them instead of my circumstances. The book of Psalms and Proverbs contain promises encouraging us to rest in the Lord and wait patiently for Him. One of my favorite verses is, "A man's heart plans his way, but the lord directs his steps" (Proverbs 16:9, NKJV). This verse shows how far God is ahead of us in His plan and His timing. He knows the end from the beginning. In His own amazing, divine way, somehow He orchestrates the decisions and events of our lives into His divine plan.

Another Miracle of Timing

I want to encourage you with one more story that I feel I must include about God's timing and His ability to intimately orchestrate all the events in our lives in a way that is beyond our capacity. Somehow He does this, working in partnership with us, but He never violates our free will. When I married my wife Caryn, she had never been married before and had no children. Even though I had five children and lost one, (my 10 year old daughter, Joanna), I had assured Caryn that if she wanted children, we would have more. As time went on, however, Caryn remained childless. After a number of years, we slowly came to the realization that maybe we might not have any children. Then, an interesting situation came across our path. A single mother we knew of in another state lost custody of her child. Through a series of events, Child Protective Services (CPS) offered custody of the baby to us. If we could not take the baby, she would become a ward of the state. Caryn jumped at the opportunity to foster this baby. I agreed. We had been uncertain about having children, even though we had done nothing to prevent it. We had left it up to the hand of the Lord. This would be a perfect opportunity for Caryn to experience motherhood, even though she didn't have a child of her own. Also, we would be rescuing a baby and helping a troubled mother.

And so it was, that a little baby girl, who we will call Mia, was unceremoniously dropped off at our house one afternoon with six garbage bags full of clothes, some baby bottles, and a little formula. Just like that, Caryn was introduced to the world of motherhood. After several rough months of adjustment to the new world of parenting, (sleepless nights, dirty diapers, etc.), we grew to love this beautiful little girl. We cuddled her and raised her for about a year. Even though my other children were grown up, I went back to being daddy, bouncing her on my lap every morning and feeding her Jell-O and treats. Caryn thrived on motherhood. She really grew in every way during this time. Also, in the backdrop of this whole scene, there was some question in our minds concerning the child's future. As time progressed, we couldn't help but wonder whether or not we might end up with this child permanently. Perhaps this was God's plan for us to become parents.

As time went on however, we slowly began to realize that this was not to be the case. Mia's mother put some of her troubles behind her and moved from another state to our state. She found herself a boyfriend and began to communicate with us and the legal system about getting her child back into her care. We could tell she mistrusted us and that she was under the impression that we were trying to steal her child. We loved little Mia, but that was not remotely true. We spoke to her and proposed a transition time to get Mia back into her care by following the normal protocol of gradually transitioning the little girl back to her mother and her new environment and living situation with minimal trauma or stress. But the mother secured a court order to immediately get her baby back. To this day, I do not know what she told the court. All I know is that she showed up one night in an old van, with paperwork and her boyfriend, and simply took everything. The boyfriend took the baby girl from us and just walked out of the house, with little Mia staring back at us over his shoulder like a deer in headlights, with this wild look that seemed to be asking, "What's happening? Where am I going?" And just like that, she was gone.

This was a form of pain I had never felt before. I felt like my guts had been ripped out. Caryn was totally devastated. The only small amount of comfort that I could find in it at all came from remembering an event that happened the night we found out the mother was coming to pick Mia up. Caryn and I sat tearfully on the couch, praying about the whole thing and committing Mia to the Lord. We had poured our lives into building love and security into this little girl's life. As we prayed, something very special and spiritual happened; we had a real God moment. Caryn did something amazing that I didn't know about and wasn't expecting. To share with you what she did, I have to give you a little bit of backstory.

Earlier in her life, before Caryn and I met, she had come to a real crossroads in her life and was very concerned and anxious about her future (marriage, family, career, ministry, etc.) One night at church, after a Bible study, Caryn shared her anxieties about the future with a lady who had made a significant spiritual impact on her life. The lady had an amazing word from God for Caryn concerning her life and future. It went something like this: she said, "Your life is preserved—set aside—as if it were in a crystal egg. It's like there's a bubble around you, protecting you, keeping you, reserving you for some specific purpose that God has for you to fulfill." Caryn knew God was speaking to her through this trusted friend and giving her comfort and peace concerning her future. She received that word and it impacted her life, her decisions, and everything she did from there on out. Now, here the two of us sat in a heart-rending moment, committing the little girl we loved and cared about to God as she was facing a very uncertain future. In a tearful moment, Caryn prayed and said, "God I take the crystal bubble that you preserved me in for Your purposes and I transfer it to Mia. I place her in that bubble of Your protection. Preserve her and reserve her for Your purposes; Your will be done in her life." I tell you, it was a very spiritual God moment; only Caryn had the right and the ability to do this. I believe she did it directly under the leading of the Holy Spirit. No matter what happens to that little girl, I believe God will preserve her for His purposes, and that our role in her life was key in connecting her to everything God has for her in the future.

As beautiful and dynamic as that moment had been, though, it brought no immediate comfort to the pain we were feeling at the abrupt loss of Mia from our household. The way it had gone down was rude, cold, and heartless. There were no thanks, no gratitude for the care we had given...nothing. I think all that added to the level of pain we were feeling. I was somewhat familiar with how to deal with loss and navigate through it. I tried to give Caryn some pointers and follow them myself. But it was no use. Caryn found a little teddy bear that had been left behind and just went and sat in the baby's room and cried and cried. To top it all off, it was the night before Christmas Eve. All the lights were up. The tree was decorated, but our hearts and our house were empty. I felt momentarily like Ebenezer Scrooge (Merry Christmas and God bless us, everyone? Bah! Humbug!) To complicate things even more, Caryn's entire family from out of town was coming over to celebrate Christmas the very next day. We had to steel ourselves with everything we had, bolster ourselves up, and entertain a full-blown family event the next day.

That following night, after everyone left, Caryn found the teddy bear and went back into the baby's room and cried some more, while I went out to get some groceries. While I was in the grocery store, I walked by the pharmaceutical aisle to buy some vitamins. I noticed a stack of pregnancy tests on the shelf by the vitamins. I literally heard a voice inside me say, "Buy one of those tests." I immediately dismissed the thought and shoved it out of my mind, thinking, "Boy Doug, now you are really going crazy, grasping at straws like that." On top of that, there was very little chance that could have been true, due to the trauma of what we had been through in the past month or two. Romance had really been the last thing on our minds during this period of time. I cashed out and drove home, but the feeling of that voice was so strong that halfway home I turned around and drove back to the grocery store. I bought the pregnancy test, along with a soda—feeling very sheepish, like an embarrassed teenager who had done something wrong.

I went back home and Caryn walked upstairs from the baby's room, her eyes red from crying. I handed her the pregnancy test and said, "Here, take this." She looked at me like I was some kind of freak. Half shocked and half angry, she stared at me and said, "What is the meaning of all this? What are you trying to do to me?" I said, "Don't ask questions. Just go in the bathroom and take it." She walked into the bathroom somewhat angrily and there was silence. Then, a minute or two later, she appeared with a wild look of shock and amazement on her face. She was pregnant. It took a few moments for what had just happened to sink in: a divine appointment in the grocery store, where a man had actually heard God say, "Buy a pregnancy test." That alone was a miracle in itself. And then the startling fact that on the very day after a heart-rending loss of losing a baby, God was giving us a child of our own. We were blown away, to say the least. We went from the pit of pain and heart-rending loss to the heights of excitement and joy.

The timing of all of this, and the circumstances surrounding it, were nothing short of miraculous, with a storybook plot line. Eight months later, our wonderful little boy, Carter, was born. We nicknamed him "the joy boy." Starting with his siblings, everyone who knows him loves him. He is a very special little guy. Once again, the reason I have shared these stories with you is to illustrate the theme of this book. The entire year that we had little Mia was very hard and very trying, with emotional, rollercoaster highs and lows: sleeplessness, major life adjustments, dealing with out of sync family members. We were introduced to the world of blended families and the challenges they present, not to speak of dealing with the legal system. But in it all, we had embraced what God led us to do and endured all the trouble, discomfort, and adjustment that, as I look back, was very trying and quite painful. The good news is that as a pastor, I learned a great deal about blended families, adoption, foster parenting, and how the legal system relates to it all. This has been invaluable for me in areas of counseling and understanding what people go through. On top of it all, we had experienced a new, valuable lesson of God's incredible and intimate involvement in our lives in absolutely every area. We developed a fresh appreciation for His meticulous timing and His miraculous provision.

Do not allow the enemy to lie to you in your mind or discourage you. We must always trust God and rest in His divine timing and know that He is intimately involved with our lives. Truly, as the Psalmist said...our times are in His hands.

Chapter 8 - A Recipe For Life

I want to give you a scripture verse that contains a three-part recipe that will help you navigate anything you are going through and find God's provision of grace on the other side. I have used this three-point directive for years as a simple navigational tool for my life. I first heard it from Derek Prince, author and Bible teacher and a former professor at Harvard University. Psalm 37:5 (NKJV) says, "Commit Your way to the Lord, trust also in Him, and He will bring it to pass." The first two things in this verse we do. The last thing is up to God. First, we commit. It's like taking your money and putting it in the bank. It is still your money, but it is in someone else's hands, under their control. Secondly, you trust. Once your money is in the bank, you don't worry about it every day—or at least you shouldn't. You go about your affairs. It's in someone else's hands and you trust that it is being properly used, cared for, and watched over. Lastly, when you really need it, it will be there with interest and increased value.

I encourage you to do this with your life or with any circumstance you are going through. First, commit it to God. Give Him control. Another verse in this vein is 1 Peter 5:7 (NIV): "Cast all your anxiety on Him because He cares for you." Once you have actually committed things to God, then trust in Him in an ongoing way. Leave it in His hands. Absolutely refuse to worry about it. Don't fret about it. Don't maneuver things in your own way. Philippians 4:6 tells us not to worry about anything; instead, pray about everything. This verse tells us to do this in every situation. I can honestly say that I have done this with my life in virtually every area. It is pretty much worry free, in matters with the church, relationships, family, finances, etc. This is a wonderful way to live. I challenge you to take a couple of the scripture verses that I have shared with you. Put them in your car. Put them on your iPad. Put them on the refrigerator. Put them in the office at work. There is a divine, spiritual ingredient and power in these verses. Memorize them; train your mind and your thinking process to do this. It is not mind over matter. This is a spiritual thing with power to bring great peace, with new perspective and direction as well.

Proverbs 23:7a says, "As a man thinks in his heart, so is he." How we think determines what we will become, and what we will do. We need to develop a Godly perspective and an understanding of what God wants for every area of our lives. We can only get that from reading and memorizing His word. We can start by committing or recommitting our lives and our future and any specific care or worry about anything to God. I guarantee you, He is not worried about anything, and neither should we be, if we are in His will and way.

I love a story in the book of Acts that demonstrates this. The apostle Peter was imprisoned for his faith by wicked King Herod, who had just beheaded James, the brother of Jesus. Peter was about to be executed himself. He was in the deepest inner prison, chained to two guards, with the doors locked: no way to escape. Yet Peter was at perfect peace. He knew he was in the center of God's will. He was snoring peacefully between two guards: sleeping so peacefully that he needed an angel to wake him up before he could rescue him. When our lives are in God's hands and we are in His will, no matter how desperate or grievous a situation we are in, we can be at perfect peace, knowing that He is in charge of our affairs. 2 Peter 1:4 tells us that God gives us precious promises from His word that allow us to be partakers of His divine nature. God wants us worry free, filled with peace, free from care, and trusting totally in Him as He orchestrates the events and situations in our lives.

I believe this exercise I have just given you is extremely important, especially when we are at a crossroads in our life. Train yourself and retrain yourself, until the directives in God's Word become part of your own mindset...until it becomes the way you think and it dictates what you do. 1 Corinthians 2:16 says, "...we have the mind of Christ." That means we have the capability to hear God speaking in our conscience and to discern spiritual things. We are told in another place to "put on the mind of Christ," or to "have the mind of Christ." This implies that even though we have that innate capability, we must develop it by retraining our minds to start thinking the way God thinks. When we achieve this, we will naturally begin to do what He would do, say what He would say, and go where He would go.

The last point in this three-part recipe is the easy and the fun one. This part is totally up to God and it's very exciting to see how He makes a way for us, provides for, and answers us. I have shared a number of stories with you to show just how true this has been in my own life. The exact same thing is true for you. As you walk in this process, you will feel a unique connection to God as your father and a special blessing when He comes through for you in any area. Because we have gone to Him and followed what He would have us do, we will know for sure that the results and things that happen in our lives are a direct result of His divine Intervention in our daily affairs. Philippians 2:13 (NIV) states that "For it is God who works in you to will and to act in order to fulfill His good purpose."

Chapter 9 - A Silver Bullet

When I was a little boy, I watched a TV show called *The Lone Ranger*. The Lone Ranger was a masked man who went around the Western United States with his Indian friend, Tonto, rescuing people. He was always doing good things like helping apprehend criminals who were harming people and destroying property. Occasionally, he would get in a real sticky situation that was threatening him and his partner. When this happened, he would pull out his gun and load it with some ammunition that had a very special feature. His bullets were made out of silver. When this special type of bullet was loaded in his gun, it always hit its target; he never missed. This made him invincible. I don't know if you are aware of this or not, but we each have a special silver bullet in our possession as well, no matter what situation you may find yourself in, no matter what the trial, or what circumstances you encounter. It doesn't even matter whether the trouble was caused by you or your own mistakes and failures. When you use your silver bullet and fire it in any situation, you will always hit your target. You will not miss, and you will win every time. **Using your silver bullet is your Godly right response and action in any situation.** This is a bullet only you can fire. To load it requires a decision of your will. It is a decision to align yourself with God's will and His Word and do whatever that requires. When you fire this bullet, you will win every time.

I know I've been using the metaphor of a silver bullet; however, in reality, the Word of God—which reveals the will of God—is your silver bullet. The Word of God never, ever misses. It always hits what it's aiming at. In Isaiah 55:11 (NIV) God says, "So is My word that goes out from My mouth: It will not return to Me empty, but will accomplish what I desire and achieve the purpose for which I sent it." At the outset of His public ministry, Jesus fired a silver bullet from the Word of God three times with great effect when he was tempted in every major area that we are faced with. Three different times Satan tried to tempt Him in the area of the desires of the flesh: hunger, thirst, a lust for power, wealth, and position. Lastly, Satan tried to get Him to supposedly prove that the Word of God is true by getting Jesus to claim some promise on His own initiative, for His own ends. (By the way, this is something we have a tendency to do many times ourselves without realizing it). But the Word of God was not on trial and Jesus was not interested in proving anything from the Word of God to Satan. The devil already knew it was true. He was just trying to put Jesus on the defensive and manipulate Him. Jesus responded three times with, "It is written...

"Man shall not live by bread alone but by every word that proceeds from the mouth of God." Then, "It is written: you should worship the Lord God only and Him only shall you serve." And when Satan tempted Him to use a scripture verse and a promise to manipulate God in His own personal situation, Jesus said, "It is written: you shall not tempt the Lord your God." (See Matthew 4:4-10). In each situation, He fired a powerful directive from the Word of God back at Satan, which completely annulled the temptation and the attack and kept Him on track.

I want to say it again. You have a silver bullet. It is your Godly right response and action in any situation. The power of this bullet comes from the alignment of your will with God's Word and God's will. Once that decision is made, you enforce it by saying it and doing it. That means firing the silver bullet of forgiveness instead of holding a grudge or getting even. It requires firing the silver bullet of giving thanks instead of grumbling and complaining. It requires the silver bullet of integrity and moral purity when we are confronted with opportunities to do the opposite.

I recently delivered a sermon called, "I am not that Man." As part of the message, I passed out rubber band bracelets that simply said, "I am not that man." The bracelets served as a visual reminder that the enemy tries to get us to live in our past with old thought patterns. He tries to accuse us, especially in our areas of weakness. He says to us, "This is how you are. This is *who* you are. The thoughts in your head are yours. And on top of that, there are feelings to go along with them. This is you. Just face the fact and go with it. You can't change. You never will. The apple doesn't fall far from the tree," and on and on and on. The thoughts flow through your mind like a badly polluted river. I tell you, when this happens, you are being attacked by the enemy in your mind, and he is trying to derail you. We must follow the instructions in the Word of God which says, in 2 Corinthians 5:17 (NIV): "Therefore, if anyone is in Christ, the new creation has come: The old has gone, the new is here!"

Furthermore, we are told to put off the old man and his sinful deeds, and put on the new man, re-created in the knowledge of Jesus Christ. When we experience these negative feelings and thought patterns, we must identify them and recognize that the enemy is trying to connect us to the guilt and failure of our past. That is no longer who we are. We must address those thoughts and we must take them captive and speak the truth over our lives instead. Arrest that thought, and fire a silver bullet. Do not let that thought define you or roam free in your mind. Instead, say what God says about you in His word. You tell the devil and yourself that the old version is no longer you. Say out loud that you are putting off the old man and his deeds and you are putting on the new man. That is how God sees you. That is how it is and that is the new you. That is the *real* you. The old man (your old sinful nature) is dead. You are no longer that man.

In Romans 12:2 (NIV), Paul tells us, "Do not conform to the pattern of this world, but be transformed by the renewing of your mind..." This means changing the way we think, and retraining our mind with new thought patterns that are in alignment with God's will and His word. Once you have been training your mind to know what God wants you to do in any given situation, you will hear God's voice in your conscience more clearly than ever, telling you the right thing to do. You will find yourself being led by the Holy Spirit on a day-to-day basis, which will bring you to a whole new level of victory and productivity in your life. But it is up to you to do the right thing (what God wants you to do). It's a decision of your will to enforce and do the will of God, even if it looks like it's going to be a disaster. Remember the main ingredient of the Lord's Prayer is, "Your kingdom come, Your will be done." Jesus further stated, when questioned about His mission on earth, "My will is to do the will of Him who sent Me." (see John 6:38). When you decide to enact God's Word and God's will in every situation and do the right thing no matter what, you will win every time. Why? Because you are enforcing the will and purpose of God in your situation. There is no higher calling, and there is no way the enemy can defeat that or stand against it, regardless of how these consequences affect you personally.

Chapter 10 - The Winning Mindset

In Daniel, Chapters 1-3, we see a story about Daniel's threes friends: Shadrach, Meshach, and Abednego. From the very start, these three young men had a Godly mindset and commitment to do what was right, no matter what the consequences. They were taken into captivity by the pagan Babylonian nation and put in a pagan environment. Despite this, they continued in their unwavering commitment to serve God and do the right thing in every situation, no matter what. One of their first challenges came when they were required to eat food that had been sacrificed to idols. It was delicious food—the best food available. But their commandant in the Old Testament law was not to eat food sacrificed to idols. So they chose to eat just plain meals, consisting of vegetables and water. When they were tested against the other young man in captivity sometime later, they were found to be healthier looking and in better shape than all the other young men who had not gone on their diet. Even though it was a diffi-cult decision to refuse to follow the directions of their captors, these young men did the right thing. As a result, they were blessed by God, and they beat the system.

Later on, the Babylonian King, Nebuchadnezzar, built a gigantic gold statue of himself and had it erected on a huge, flat field, where it could be viewed by the masses. He then got an entire troupe of musicians together to begin to play pagan music. He had representatives from all over his empire there. He issued a command, "When the music begins to play, I want all of you to get down on your knees and worship the golden statue of me. And, if you don't, you will be thrown alive into a fiery furnace and burned to death."

The people were assembled before the giant golden statue. It was quite a scene. The musicians began to play, and as they played, the whole field of people went down to their knees, paying obeisance to the fierce Babylonian ruler, except for three men, standing alone like giants in the field. The king couldn't believe his eyes. He was enraged, and he pulled the three young men out of the crowd to stand before him. He already knew these three young men and he respected them for their values and their backbone. The king was furious, but he wanted to give them another chance. He said, "Perhaps you didn't hear me, so I'm going to give you another chance. When you hear the music play again, fall down and worship the golden statue. If not, you will be thrown into the fiery furnace."

Daniel's three friends were between a rock and a hard place. It was truly an impossible situation. Their choice was either to disobey God's Word and worship a false God by obeying the king's orders, or die. Yet the three young men answered in an unwavering manner. They said, "We want you to know, o king, that regardless of the consequences, we will never bend the knee to your image. Our God is able to save us from the fiery furnace, but even if He doesn't, we will never worship it." (See Daniel 3:16-18). The king was enraged. He told his men to heat the fiery furnace seven times hotter than it already was and throw the non-conformists in. Daniel's three friends had fired a silver bullet (they had done the right thing). Now, it had them facing the worst possible consequence. The king's strongest men threw them into the fire. The fire was so hot by this point, that all of the soldiers who were involved in throwing them into the furnace were killed by the extreme heat. Shortly after this took place, the king saw something that totally blew his mind. As he peered into the furnace, he saw Daniel's three friends walking around, alive in the fire. On top of that, there was a fourth figure in the fire — a shining, brilliant figure unlike the other three. The reason we know this is because the king even commented in astonishment and said, "The fourth one looks like the son of God." (See Daniel 3:25). The king went as near as he could to the over-heated furnace and shouted, "Shadrach, Meshach, and Abednego, come out of the fire!" They came out and stood before the king. They were unharmed. Their clothes were unharmed. They didn't even smell like smoke. Only one thing had been burned; the cords that bound them and held them captive had all burned off them, and they were free.

Commitment is Key

There are some amazing lessons here for us. First and foremost, I would comment on the mindset of these young men. They were interested primarily in doing the right thing, regardless of the consequences. Remember, they did not know how this was going to turn out, which brings me to another scary point. There were three ways for God to deliver them, just as there are three ways God can deliver you. God can save you *from* the fire or He can save you *in* the fire. He can also save you *through* the fire. God could've kept those men from even getting into this challenging situation, thereby saving them *from* the fire. But God chose to save them *in* the fire, as he kept them from suffering any physical harm. Had He chosen to, God could have allowed them to die, standing for His purposes as many have throughout history. Even though they may have died a painful death, His plan of redemption would have drawn them—through their obedience and His grace—to eternal life with Him. This would be the option of saving them *through* the fire.

In any case, we must be confident that God has a personal plan for us that will work out for our good and for His kingdom, no matter what happens in our particular situation. Daniel's three friends knew the way to go was to obey God's Word and do the right thing. This understanding went much deeper than emotions. This was something deep and spiritual. The key concept here was illustrated by them when they said, "Even if God does not deliver us, we won't do the wrong thing." Their mindset was that they were going to stand for God and what was right, because it wasn't about them. Something greater was at stake. These were not weak, needy men. It wasn't about them at all. They truly had it right. They knew something much bigger and greater was at stake than their personal comfort or even their own rescue. These men were not double minded or self centered. They had one core value, one thing they stood for: to do the will of God. They were going to do the right thing, no matter what. This is the way we need to be. This is what we need to do in our own lives.

Sooner or later, everyone faces a critical point in their life in some area where they are overwhelmingly tempted to compromise, go the wrong way, or do the wrong thing. Maybe this whole scenario is being played out in your life as you are reading right now. It is imperative that we make the right choice. I will tell you something else that is very important to know. Many times these challenges come at critical points in our lives and the decisions we make will dramatically affect the quality and the impact of our lives and future. Follow God's leading in your conscience. ***Do the right thing.***

Now I would like to look at the end result of this entire story. The bottom line was that there was a giant spiritual battle being waged behind the scenes in the spiritual world that played out in our tangible world. The question at stake: Who is God, and who is in control? Because Daniel's three friends stood for God and God's purposes, that question was answered in the physical world. God is in control of human affairs and He is represented by those who serve Him.

Because of their stand, shockwaves reverberated in the unseen world. A tremendous spiritual battle was won that changed the entire atmosphere of the Babylonian kingdom. Demonic forces behind the scenes were completely shut down by the decision of Daniel's three friends to stand for God and His word. This story clearly shows our partnership with God and the importance of our decisions. Our decisions to do the right thing, based on God's Word, have tremendous spiritual power and implications. King Nebuchadnezzar stated publicly, "Now I know that your God is the only true God. Because there is no God that can deliver anyone like this." That became the new standard for the Kingdom of Babylon. The King wrote letters and sent them to the four corners of this kingdom saying, "People everywhere need to honor the God of Shadrach, Meshach, and Abednego. If they don't, they will be cut in pieces, and their homes will be turned into dunghills." Even though the Jewish people were captives in a foreign land, they were now respected and looked up to. The true God's existence and His control over human affairs was established in what had been a pagan, fallen society.

Finally, Daniel's three friends had a personal, dynamic, deep spiritual encounter with the Lord of the universe, and guess where they met Him? They met Him in the fire. They came out of that fire and that dark, trying time smelling like a rose. They were free from their bonds, with a deeper respect and revelation of who God is in a very personal sense. This is another reason why God allows us to go through hard times, painful times, and struggles, collectively referred to as "the fire." Remember the title of this book. The dark side of faith is this: God is willing to let you suffer and go through difficult times that can be very trying and hard. His purpose in this is to build His kingdom in and through you. No matter what you are going through, God is always positioning your life: orchestrating both the good and the bad to set up your life to make an impact for His kingdom and His glory. Further, He wants to shape godly character in you. As we deny choosing a self-centered existence and what's seemingly good for us, and make it all about Him and what His will and purpose is, we become like Him. We find ourselves orbiting His purposes, His universe, His will, and His plan. It becomes the supreme reason for our existence.

As I stated before, many Christians still have a self-centered sense of existence, living a life of their choice and trying to use God's promises to order their world the way they envision it. Eventually, though, this self-centered mindset does not work in the kingdom of God. If we try to live that way, eventually we will get stuck or discouraged or even offended when things just aren't working. It's high time to get back to the true center of every believer's universe (**Your kingdom come, Your will be done**—regardless of the consequences). If you are stuck right now between a rock and a hard place, I would like to tell you that you need to do what Daniel's three friends did. In order to navigate your difficult situation and circumstance, you need to make a decision to do the right thing. Push aside feelings and emotions and just do the right thing—and you will win every time. Even if you are hurt, or it's painful and there are consequences, do not let that stop you from doing the right thing. There is more at stake with you and your decisions than meets the eye, just as there was in the world of Shadrach, Meshach, and Abednego. The same war is going on in your personal world and your sphere of influence. The decisions you make have far greater implications than you and I can see.

If you're offended, in a compromising situation of some sort, or you're just plain stuck and don't know which way to turn or which way to go, commit your entire situation and condition to God and say, "God, this is where I am. This is what's going on. This is what I would love to see, but, regardless of all that, Your kingdom come, Your will be done in my life. Show me Your will and Your way, and I will walk in it." If you yield in this way, you will reset your entire compass. You will bring yourself into alignment with God's purpose and plan for you. Great peace will flood your soul as you recalibrate and find your center.

Finding the Answers

Next, identify the true nature of whatever situation you are in and go straight to God's Word for direction. The promises and directives in the Word of God are alive with a hidden spiritual power that will set you free and empower you to do the right thing. Jesus said, in John 6:63 (NKJV), "...The words I speak to you are spirit, and they are life." The key to tapping the spiritual power in the Word of God is first of all believing it, and secondly obeying it.

Faith + obedience = power

John 1:12 (KJV) says, "But as many as received Him, to them He gave power to become the sons of God, even to them that believe on His name." You may say, "I'm no Bible scholar...I don't know what verses to read. I don't know what stories to read." Just Google the keyword that describes your situation. If it's fear that has gripped you, Google Bible verses for overcoming fear. If it's a moral dilemma, Google "Bible directives for morality." Other key areas might be "...raising children," "financial direction," or "decisions about the future." When you've found the verses that correspond to and provide answers for your situation, write them down, and plaster them all over your refrigerator, your steering wheel, and your iPhone. Put sticky notes on your desk. Memorize those verses. Retrain your mind. If you don't have a computer or any technology skills, get a friend to do it for you or find some other way, but do not be lazy. Take charge of your life and the direction for your life and be responsible. The Bible is the roadmap for your life and how you are to live. Proverbs 4:20-22 (NIV) says, "My son, pay attention to what I say; turn your ear to My words. Do not let them out of your sight, keep them within your heart; for they are life to those who find them and health to one's whole body."

Once you have decided to do the will of God and obey the Word of God, you will hear Him speaking to you in your conscience...your spirit. You will hear His still, small voice. It is important that you listen to what He is telling you there. Along with that, God will guide you through circumstances, and through divine appointments with the people you meet. As time goes on, you will find yourself unstuck, with a fresh sense of peace and wholeness. You will find yourself on a new path of purpose that will flood your life with new energy, because you exist for something much bigger and grander than yourself. It's the very reason you were created. Suddenly, you will begin to recognize God's hand in everything—every little thing. Even in the tough and trying times. You will see how everything works together in shaping you and positioning you to do God's will and to make you like Him.

Something else happens that is amazing when we see our true purpose and began to embrace God's will and plan for us. There comes this new, dynamic passion and zeal for life and the future that comes from somewhere outside ourselves, mainly from the indwelling Spirit of God Himself. A divine energy lights up our life with a new attitude and renewed strength that says, "Bring out the lions and heat up the fire." It's a supernatural, spiritual strength. The book of Isaiah says it well: "He gives strength to the weary and increases the power of the weak. Even youths grow tired and weary, and young men stumble and fall; but those who hope in the lord will renew their strength. They will soar on wings like eagles; they will run and not grow weary, they will walk and not be faint" (Isaiah 40:29-31, NIV).

I invite you to pray this prayer: Lord, I commit my entire situation to you. I will obey Your Word and Your voice speaking to my conscience. I will do the right thing, no matter what the cost, no matter what the consequences are. I will trust You to bring me through this and work it all out for good for Your kingdom, Your glory, and my future as well.

Chapter 11 - Go the Distance

James 1:2-4 (NIV) says, "Consider it pure joy my brothers and sisters, whenever you face trials of many kinds, because you know that the testing of your faith produces perseverance. Let perseverance finish its work so that you may be mature and complete, not lacking anything."

There is an ingredient which, when added to our faith and obedience, really gets the job done. Again, in keeping with the title of this book, the addition of this ingredient is not too often an enjoyable experience; it is called "perseverance." Some Bible translations call it "patience." I might use these terms interchangeably, in that they do mean the same thing. The definition of these two words is "...the ability to hang on and go the distance." As the definition implies, many times the exercise of patience or perseverance may entail a good deal of waiting.

I will give you an example of what I am talking about from my experience. I am a hunter. I love bow hunting particularly. (Forgive me, any of you who are Vegans or anti-hunters and who may be reading this. If it makes you feel any better, I want you to know that we actually eat any wild game or fish that we harvest, with the exception of what we donate to food pantries on a fairly regular basis.) One icy cold morning, I was sitting deep in a swampy woods. There were several inches of snow on the ground and it was bitterly cold, down near zero. I had crept into my favorite spot well before daylight to get the jump on everything and everyone. I figured that doing this would set me up so that any late-coming hunters would make noise and push the deer back to where I already was. Much to my dismay, though, just as daylight came, I heard breaking branches and crunching snow as two different hunters came from opposite directions and sat down within sight of me. This was not the way I had envisioned things going. And, because they did not keep an appropriate distance from where I was positioned, I held the distinct impression that this was a bit rude, but I just sat there in dismay. My formerly intimate spot and my master plan were ruined. I was tempted to hang it up and leave. On top of that, the brutal cold was starting to get to me, as I had been there for over an hour already. Then I thought of the only way to keep my plan alive and preserve everything I had done; I decided that I would simply outlast these two other hunters. I would endure the cold and outlast them. I knew there were many deer around, and when these interloping hunters left as noisily as they had come, there was still a decent chance they would push deer that would sneak around behind them and then come my way.

The morning wore on and I became freezing cold. But, I was well-dressed, so I gritted my teeth and just hung on. Why? Because I believed in my plan. I knew I was in the right place and I knew endurance and patience could present me with an opportunity for success. My plan did ultimately work. After a long sit, first one hunter got up and left; then, finally, the last hunter got up and crunched noisily away. I watched in the direction he had left very carefully and sure enough, five to seven minutes later, a nice buck snuck out of the thicket in his back trail and stood watching intently in the direction the hunter had gone. Needless to say, I harvested the unsuspecting buck. I don't know if I was more elated by bagging a good-sized deer or by the fact that my plan had worked. The lesson I would like to draw from the story is very clear. Once we have a proper perspective of God and what He wants for us and we do the right thing, we need to hang on and have endurance while God works things out. We must determine to go the distance and hang on.

Patience (endurance) is a key ingredient in our lives. It keeps our faith out there working. We believe God, we act on what we believe, and then we put forth the effort to endure, working with faith until God brings it all to pass. The Bible states the truth of this so very clearly in Hebrews 10:36 (NIV), where it says, "You need to persevere so that when you have done the will of God, you will receive what He has promised." We must determine never to quit, never to give up. Almost everyone knows Winston Churchill's famous speech to a graduating class in England. It was short, powerful, and to the point. He stood up and proclaimed in a loud voice: "Never give up! Never give up! Never give up!" and then he sat back down. My father had a similar motto for his life that I continue to carry with me today. I remember it well. He said, "I refuse to be taken out of the game. I refuse to be benched. I refuse to be polarized to where I can do nothing." His life backed up his motto.

Detours Lead to Destinations

Sometimes we can experience a great tragedy or an unforeseen situation that just seems to stop us dead in our tracks. Other times, we may experience a long flat-line in our day-to-day existence, where almost nothing seems to ever change or happen. Either of these things can tend to drain us of our energy and bring disappointment and for some, even depression. As I am writing this, something specific that illustrates this concept comes to my mind...the thing that triggered me in the writing of this book. I had just been asked to go to overseas to be one the principal speakers at what potentially was to be one of the largest pastors' conferences in India's history. They were expecting up to 15,000 pastors from all over India. On top of that, a person who I greatly admired, Dr. Paul Yongi Cho, (Senior Pastor of the one million member church in Seoul, South Korea), was to be the principal speaker at the related crusade campaign and I was told that I would possibly get to be the primary speaker one night of the crusade as well. The organizers of this event were expecting a million people to attend a crusade.

To put this opportunity in a bit more context, I had been to India several times before. In fact, many years earlier, God had given me a special love for India and a burden to help reach that nation. I expected this trip to be the highlight of my life. It would be an opportunity to contribute to making a massive spiritual impact on a nation. I fasted. I prayed. I prepared. Then I received some very disappointing news. I and others who were invited from outside the country had our visa requests refused. I learned later that one of the reasons may have been that some high-ranking Hindu ministers and officials disputed the crusade and our right to come into their country. After the original denial of my request, I drove to Chicago and tried to resubmit paperwork for the visa. I was told that my particular visa request was for a special type of visa reserved for dignitaries, high-profile people, speakers, etc. They restated to me that my request had already been refused and that they could do nothing about it at their level. I went home somewhat devastated, and I was tempted to be depressed, which would be a big thing for me. People who know me, know that I don't get depressed. I sat at home and thought, "What am I going to do now? I have all this fire, all this energy, all this prayer and preparation. I am not going to do nothing. God, what do You want me to do?"

Then a thought came to me, "You have been planning to write a book for years...why don't you start?" I knew instantly it was a God thought. My next thought was, "If I can't bless people with the truth of God's Word one way, I'll do it another way." Right then and there, I decided I was going to start writing the book I'd been thinking about for years. I shoved aside my pain, disappointment, and frustration and I sat down that very day to begin writing. And, as if this new-found window of opportunity was not enough, as I was writing this book, I received inspiration and ideas for two more books. I want to say it again: never quit; never give up; go the distance. Figure out how to be a blessing and how to bring life in any situation you are in. If you can't do it one way, pray for Godly inspiration to do it another way — and never quit.

I will give you another example of being flexible in finding a way to serve the purposes God has for your life. I had been in leadership roles for years. I was a leader in business, a leader in my home, a leader in the church. With respect to my church, I was the worship leader, an elder, and a Bible teacher. At a certain point in our local church's development, the elders decided to go a certain direction that I was not comfortable with. I will never forget the day I simply had to lay everything down and give God my ministry. No one forced me to do this; I just felt that was what God was asking me to do. I quietly resigned from my official position and privately told the office assistant who did payroll to quit paying me my part-time salary. I continued to serve as a volunteer in leading worship and whatever else my duties required. A short time later, I felt God releasing me from my ministry at that church. When I felt the release to leave, I left without any fuss.

This was a very sad moment for me, because my father had started that church and it had become very influential in the area. As he led the church, I had stayed by his side from day one, assisting him. When he passed away, a lot of things changed, as they usually do when a mainstay leader leaves or dies. Shortly after my departure, a number of other families left that church as well. They began meeting midweek to pray and fellowship, and to figure out where to go and what to do next. There was a general consensus among them that they would like to start a new church. I did not feel a personal leading to start a new church at that time. A number of the people who had gathered together were hurting and somewhat mistrusting of church leadership. This was very understandable, considering what they had been through, as they had invested themselves in an organization that decided to change direction without their input. Everyone was a bit gun shy. My biggest concern was that they would embrace some of the same things that had contributed to dividing the last church they were in. But the Holy Spirit challenged me with a question I wasn't particularly excited about answering. He asked, "Are you willing to put the needs of these people in their current situation ahead of your own plans and desires?" I remember that tears were running down my face when I said "Yes" (and I seldom cry). Then He said, "Well, then, help them."

The original group quickly grew in numbers to several dozen people. So we rented a facility and started having services. I led worship, preached, and shared leadership responsibilities in planting this young, new congregation.

After not too long a period of time, the church reached approximately 200 people. They elected elders and established an official direction and goal. Incidentally, my younger brother, Calvin, became the lead elder and eventually the senior pastor of that church, and it is thriving and growing to this day.

A Different Kind of Leadership

Once things were up and running with the new church plant, our family began attending Resurrection Life Church in Grandville, Michigan. I sat in the audience feeling quite strange...no position, no leadership role—everything was changed, and there I sat. It was a hard time for both me and my family. We had been through over two years of transition: changing churches; starting a new church; leaving friends and family. It would have been very easy for me to fall back and develop a settled existence, (tired and inactive).

At this point, I would like to say something to you that is very important. Remember what I stated earlier, that God is always positioning us, always teaching us, always refining us, always moving us ever forward in our twofold purpose? When we go through transition or encounter difficult stretches in our journey, we need to hang on, hold on, endure, wait patiently, and don't give up. Also in these times, it's very important to recognize the season we are in and embrace it. We must try to learn as much as we can. Never stop learning; never stop trying; never allow a mindset that settles for good enough.

Sometimes, as we grow older, there is a tendency to develop a mentality that we have peaked or that we are past our prime. This is a huge mistake. Every day, every moment of our lives, is valuable. Don't waste it. Ronald Reagan became president of the United States at 69 years old. He was just entering his most productive years on this planet. President Theodore Roosevelt was found dead in his bed at the age of 65, reading a self-improvement book. Don't ever settle, don't ever quit. Don't complain or be frustrated. Instead, look around and ask, "God, what do You want me to see? What do You want me to do?" Remember, God is using everything to prepare you for what's ahead.

Not too long after joining Resurrection Life Church, I was invited to play guitar in the band. I became a rank and file member of the team. Here, God had another lesson for me to learn. That lesson was how to lead from the back row. I had been a worship leader for almost 20 years, calling all the shots, fronting the band, deciding what to do when and where. Now I was on a team, taking orders and not being asked for any input on anything. On top of that, the young worship leader was less experienced than me. I noted this fact, and I so wanted to offer him some advice that I thought could improve the team in a number of areas. However, I knew that it wouldn't work without having a stronger relationship in place with him. So, I bit my tongue, dug in, and just served. As unnatural as it was for me to do so, I kept my mouth shut. As time went on, I began to learn that leadership is not as much about one's position as it is about the ability to influence people. I realized that was what God wanted to teach me, and I began to make as dynamic a contribution from my place on the team as I could. I never missed a practice or a service for six years, unless I was officially on vacation. I really learned how to influence, bless, and contribute to the quality and direction of our team without undermining the leader and without having a leadership position.

As a side note, I also discovered how God must feel when He sits at the top of the universe and has at His disposal everything He needs to do anything He desires. He watches us use our free will to navigate and watches our bumbling and our mistakes. But He does not violate our free will. Instead, very carefully, He orchestrates certain things, certain events, to impact and move us. Gradually and slowly, He leads us into the right vein. I found that this type of approach takes a great deal of patience and a great deal of wisdom. I gained a much greater respect and appreciation for how God deals with us when—though He can absolutely do anything—He patiently goes at our speed, and limits Himself to a partnership with flawed you and me, until we learn and come up to speed.

I went on to learn so many things from the back row. The church I had joined was a very large church, with thousands of people. I grew to understand the infrastructure of this large of an organization, with both its strengths and its weaknesses. I learned a lot more about what it feels like to be a volunteer. I learned how to keep a good attitude as a volunteer. Volunteers are the lifeblood of any vital, active, healthy, growing church. Even the very best churches with good-sized budgets can have only a small amount of staff, compared to the large number of volunteers needed to run a local church. During this time, I learned first-hand about their struggles and scheduling conflicts. (By the way, I believe there is a special reward for those who serve without pay and without position, ever existing to build the kingdom of God and bless God's people.) All in all, the experiences I had during that time continue to help me a lot today as a leader. In addition, during that time the foundation was laid for me to move into everything I am involved in to this present day.

Finish Your Race

I'm sure some of you reading this are facing some real challenges and difficult situations. Stand on the promises in God's Word. He will make a way where there is no way. Read Isaiah 43, meditate on it, and then ask God to make a way for you; then just hang on. Embrace your season. Learn everything you can—you will need it later. Be patient, endure, and follow the inner witness of what God is telling you to do. The Hebrew writer starts his wrap-up of the book with a challenge to run the race of this life with endurance. Hebrews 12:1- 4 (NKJV) says:

> Therefore we also, since we are surrounded by so great a cloud of witnesses, let us lay aside every weight, and the sin which so easily ensnares us, and let us run with endurance the race that is set before us, [2] looking unto Jesus, the author and finisher of our faith, who for the joy that was set before Him endured the cross, despising the shame, and has sat down at the right hand of the throne of God. [3] For consider Him who endured such hostility from sinners against Himself, lest you become weary and discouraged in your souls. [4] You have not yet resisted to bloodshed, striving against sin.

We all have a cross to carry. Our cross is the will of God for our life. Not our will, but His will. Jesus said, "...if any man will come after Me, let him deny himself, and take up his cross daily, and follow Me," Luke 9:23 (KJV). The cross may include some painful and unpleasant things, as we are refined and positioned to do God's will in this life; however, if we endure, the necessary ingredient of patience will be added to our faith and will keep it out there, working until God brings the desired results to pass in our lives.

I will close this chapter with a challenge and a promise from the Word of God. James 1:4 (NIV) says, "Let perseverance finish its work so that you may be mature and complete, not lacking anything." I challenge you to identify any difficult situation in your life where you need to have endurance. Recommit that area to the Lord. Make sure you are doing all the right things at the present time and then decide to just buckle down and be faithful, and go the distance until God brings resolution in that area, regardless of how long it may take.

A Challenge for You: Google New Testament Bible verses on patience: memorize your favorite one, and read and meditate on the others. Then, listen to the voice of the Holy Spirit pointing out any area you need to grow and develop in patience, and decide to hold on and go the distance.

Chapter 12 - The Final Ingredient: Hope

Hope: "Favorable and confident expectation, a happy anticipation of good—the object of which is God" (*Vines Expository Dictionary*).

There is a final ingredient that the Bible talks about that is key to us living the life of faith. It is one of faith's closest friends. It keeps us going. It helps us survive every trial and keeps us reaching upward and onward. It is called *hope*.

There seems to be a real shortage of hope these days; there's just not a lot of it around. More and more, our whole world seems to be devoid of hope. Not too long ago I compiled some notes, statistics, and inspirational ideas for this chapter, as well as a number of quotes from Terry Law's excellent book, titled *The Hope Habit*. In it, he gives a compelling overview of everything that's going on in the world. In his chapter, "Whatever Happened to Hope?" Terry points out that many third-world countries are ravaged by famine, disease, civil war, starving children, and death. All over Europe once great cultures are dying off following centuries of godless secularism. Even here in the United States hope is taking a huge blow. The American dream, instead of being the norm, is more and more becoming an illusion for many, as they watch jobs, equity, value, and retirement accounts all go out the window. We watch TV at home and watch CEO's loot their corporations. The politicians who represent us crash and burn before our eyes. Meanwhile, most people's incomes are slowly going down while companies bailed out with our tax dollars hand out raises and bonuses to their staff. TV shows focus on sex and murder and parents have had to become security guards for their children, protecting them from stalkers, porn, and chat rooms on the Internet, not to speak of guarding them from the danger of alternative lifestyles and the occult.

For my part, even as I sit here writing this, I am watching another crisis develop in the Middle East as again we are being pulled into conflict. On top of that we are in the nuclear age and the whole world is a tinderbox. Thoughts of the end of the age and Armageddon are hanging in the air and swirling in people's heads. All of these things tend to breed anger, frustration and cynicism in people. Then, when our personal life takes a hit and our lower dream (what we hope for in this life) is damaged, it pushes us to the edge of what I will call the three D's: discouragement, despair, and depression. A sense of hopelessness replaces hope.

A Bible verse (Proverbs 13:12a) perfectly describes this condition. It says, "Hope deferred makes the heart sick" (NIV). Terry shares a perfect example of this with the following story. When the tiny nation of Latvia gained its independence in 1991, Betsy Thraves, an American missionary, went to teach English to teenagers at a language school in Riga. She asked about their goals and their dreams at the outset of the class and there was dead silence. She pushed them a bit. Still silence, except for one student who muttered something under his breath. She asked him, "What did you say?" He said, "I said, what's the use? All our hopes and dreams for good never happen anyway." Unwittingly, he had spoken for the tens of millions set free with the collapse of the communist eastern bloc. They had been set free, yet hopeless chains of despair from a half a century still hung over them. The young man said, "We wake up every day expecting things to go wrong. Then we are never disappointed. Then if anything better than the worst actually happens, it's a nice surprise" (*The Hope Habit*, pp. 47-48). I used this example because many people struggle even in our country, a land of opportunity, as over 3 million Americans suffer with chronic depression. Twenty million more suffer with various lesser types of depression, mood disorders, etc. The World Health Organization has predicted that by 2020, depression will be the second largest killer in the world (*The Hope Habit*, p. 25). The downward spiral of discouragement, despair and depression leads us to the mindset of fatalism. Fatalism defined is, what's the use? Nothing I do matters anyhow. Nothing I do is going to change things, so I will just disengage. This leads to a vain existence and a sense of worthlessness. Three of the largest world religions don't offer any help, either.

Terry goes on to explain the centerpiece of each of these three religions. Buddhism is based on the idea that the essence of life is suffering. Freedom from that is called "Nirvana," which aspires to nothingness—not happiness—and that life is just the illusion of peace that comes from nonexistence. Islam contains just as much fatalism as Buddhism. Buddhism starves the soul, while the more radical, extreme elements of Islam seem to possess a cancer of hate and revenge that devours the soul. The only ultimate guarantee of heaven is suicide: in other words, ending it all. Hinduism has institutionalized fatalism with reincarnation, which teaches that your present station in life is your wages, either good or bad, from a previous life. As Terry so pointedly summarizes it, the Hindu position is that "...not only does life stink, but you also deserve it" (*The Hope Habit*, p. 7). In fact, nothing you do can change it.

Good grief! Help, somebody...please help! Well, thank God, there *is* help. There is an antidote to fatalism. That antidote is hope. Not just any kind of hope, but a living hope, a real hope that can totally be realized. A hope that can bring you to the top of the universe and keep you there. That hope is not only for this life, but it extends into eternity and never ever fades; it actually gets brighter and brighter every day. The book of Psalms says the path of the righteous person grows brighter and brighter until the full day appears. The full day is the timelessness of eternity, a never-ending day. Every person who is a believer (those who have turned from their sins and accepted Jesus as their Savior and Lord) has true hope available to them. That hope became a reality for us when Jesus rose from the dead. In 1 Peter 1:3-4 (NIV) it says, "Praise be to the God and Father of our Lord Jesus Christ! In His great mercy He has given us new birth into a living hope through the resurrection of Jesus Christ from the dead, and into an inheritance that can never perish, spoil or fade..." The true source of hope is God, and the only way to have true hope for your life and eternity is rooted in a life that is connected to God and His purposes. All other hope is short-lived, temporal, or false hope, based on fantasy or a deception.

The Source of True Hope

The virgin birth of Jesus Christ, His life, His death and resurrection are the foundation for all true hope. His death on the cross paid for our sins and wiped our slate clean so we could stand faultless before God and have a living relationship with Him, just like Adam and Eve did in the garden. Adam and Eve were created perfect, and they walked and talked with God, but their relationship with God depended entirely upon their performance. There was no such thing as grace. There was no insurance, or as I like to say, "assurance plan" in place. If they did one thing wrong, they would be out of God's favor and subject to separation from God, and subsequent judgment.

But now, through the cross, God's grace is available to us. Grace is God's undeserved favor, which was purchased for us by all that Christ has done. The Bible says that Christ *is* our righteousness. Our relationship with God is no longer dependent on our performance, but on grace, the undeserved favor purchased for us on the cross. The work of the cross has forever removed the penalty of sin and made a right relationship with God possible. We can walk with God in a living relationship. In a sense, we can not only go back to how it was originally in the Garden of Eden, but it's even better than that. We can walk and talk with God with confidence and the security that even if we make a mistake and sin, we will not lose our relationship with God, because it is no longer based on our performance; it is based on what Christ has done for us. We are in Christ—He is our perfect performance, because we are in Him. Colossians 3:3 says that we have died to our old life, and now our lives are hid with Christ in God. 1 John 2:1 (NIV) says, "…we have an advocate with the Father." Jesus is our mediator, our representative before God on our behalf. He represents us, and God will forgive our sin, because, as the song says:

> Jesus paid it all,
> All to him I owe.
> Sin had left a crimson stain,
> He washed it white as snow.
> *("Jesus Paid It All," Elvina M. Hall, 1865)*

As we walk in the free provision of God's grace and live in His undeserved favor, there is one thing we must always remember—there is no excuse whatsoever to try to use God's grace as a license to go on living a life of sin. Grace is an exit strategy from a life of sin to live the life God originally intended us to live. As we walk the path of that new life, Romans 8:1-2 (NIV) says, "Therefore, there is now no condemnation for those who are in Christ Jesus, because through Christ Jesus the law of the Spirit who gives life has set you free from the law of sin and death." Christ's death and resurrection are the foundation for all true HOPE. Everything good that will ever happen in your life and eternity are based on this foundation alone.

If you are reading this book and you know some things about God, but you are not sure of your relationship with Him, I have good news! You can have a relationship with God that is alive. You can have true, living hope in this life and you can have eternal life. Just go to the back of this book and pray a prayer you will find there (*The End*, Prayer for Salvation); I have put this together to help you understand how to receive Christ as your Savior and become a child of God. The moment you do, peace will flood your soul as God turns the light on in your spirit, and you will *know* that you have passed from spiritual darkness and uncertainty into a life that is full of light. Your life will be directly connected to God through Jesus Christ. You will find peace for your soul. It is the doorway to a whole new beginning.

Living a Life Based Upon Hope

Now that we have established the foundation of true hope (a reality that we can count on for this life and eternity), I would like to talk about how to establish this living hope as a central ingredient in your life. First, I would like to state that ***hope is a choice.*** In the book of Psalms, King David was discouraged. He was struggling with his enemies and experiencing inner turmoil. He made an interesting statement. He asked himself the question in Psalm 42:5 (NKJV), "Why are you cast down O my soul? And why are you disquieted within me? Hope in God, for I shall yet praise Him for the help of His countenance." (Our countenance is our face, whether it is one that reflects sadness, happiness, joy, or despair). Much of the time, you can have a pretty good hint of what's going on within a person just by looking at them—their facial expression and their posture. When we are going through hard times and struggles, we have a choice to either be discouraged and hopeless, or to choose to have hope and to live in hope. You may ask, "How do I do that?" I will tell you how. Instead of meditating on how bad things are, how bad you feel, or what you are going through, immediately begin to count your blessings to keep a God-perspective in your circumstances. When I challenged my congregation to do this, I painted a picture of King David on a rainy morning, hunted by enemies, separated from his family, without the comforts of home. He stood in the opening of his dreary cave and looked into the rain and shivered. Then, to keep his perspective, he talked to himself. He told himself what to do. In Psalm 103 (NKJV), he said,

> Bless the lord, O my soul; And all that is within me, bless His holy name. [2]Bless the lord, O my soul, and forget not all His benefits: [3]Who forgives all your iniquities, Who heals all your diseases, [4]Who redeems your life from destruction, Who crowns you with loving-kindness and tender mercies, [5]Who satisfies your mouth with good things, So that your youth is renewed like the eagle's.

On and on he went...

¹⁰He has not dealt with us according to our sins, nor punished us according to our iniquities. ¹¹For as the heavens are high above the earth, So great is His mercy toward those who fear Him; ¹²As far as the east is from the west, So far has He removed our transgressions from us. ¹³As a father pities his children, so the tLORD pities those who fear Him. ¹⁴For He knows our frame; He remembers that we are dust. ¹⁵As for man, his days are like grass; As a flower of the field, so he flourishes. ¹⁶For the wind passes over it, and it is gone, And its place remembers it no more.

Now David is really rolling. He has it all in perspective; he sees his frail finiteness compared to God's infinite grace and mercy and blessing. Now he has gotten beyond himself, and his perspective switches to the dynamic God perspective on things that we all need to have. He goes on to state:

The LORD has established His throne in heaven, And His kingdom rules over all. ²⁰ Bless the LORD, you His angels, Who excel in strength, who do His word, Heeding the voice of His word. ²¹Bless the LORD, all you His hosts, You ministers of His, who do His pleasure. ²²Bless the LORD, all His works, In all places of His dominion. Bless the LORD, O my soul!

This is what you and I should strive to do: we can stop complaining and count our blessings instead. We have a hope and a purpose in this life: plus, we have eternal life forever and ever. We are becoming like Jesus. God is using all the tough things and hard things we go through to refine us and make us like Him. We are actually partners with Him, doing what He created us to do.

Choosing Hope over Despair

King David also made an interesting statement in the Old Testament when he was going through other trials and struggles. He said, "I would have lost heart unless I had believed that I would see the goodness of the Lord in the land of the living (in this life)" Psalm 27:13, (NKJV). David chose to hope. Hope is a choice. We must choose to hope. Furthermore, *hope is something that you build.* We start building hope by counting our blessings. Doing this helps us keep a God perspective. The next thing we must do to build hope is to praise and worship God. As we worship, we are saying, "God, it's all about You; You are in control."

When we choose to hope in the Lord, count our blessings and worship Him, it creates a defensive shield and launches an offensive that the enemy of our souls cannot penetrate or stand against. In the book of Acts, Paul and Silas had been called to plant a New Testament church in the city of Philippi. They were led there by God, but as they shared and preached the gospel, they ran straight into trouble. Sometimes, we think because God is leading us and we are following Him, that everything will work out just fine—and ultimately it does. But the dark side of faith sometimes entails trouble, hardship, and pain. There may be some very uncomfortable things we have to go through as we follow God and do His will.

In the process of following God's leading to plant the church in Philippi, Paul and Silas freed a young lady they met along the way from the power of an evil spirit that had enabled her to be a fortuneteller. Because they would now lose the income that her fortune-telling powers brought in, her owners were furious and had Paul and Silas publicly accused and beaten. Then they were thrown into jail and put in stocks. Things seemed hopeless. They were wounded, in pain, and locked up so they couldn't move. In spite of their circumstances, though, Paul and Silas began to worship, singing songs and hymns. As they kept their God-perspective and chose to hope in God and worship Him, God did the impossible. He caused an earthquake; the prison doors opened, the chains and stocks fell off. Not only theirs, but the other prisoners' as well. Even though there was a clear path to freedom, the prisoners did not choose to escape. Because they didn't lead a jailbreak, they were able to stay and minister to their jailer, who got saved, took them to his own home, cleaned them up, and fed them. Then the rest of the jailer's family got saved. Paul baptized them all, and that very night they *did* start the Philippian church—in the jailer's home. God made a way for them where there was no way. He will make a way for you too, but you must choose to hope in Him, count your blessings, and worship Him.

In Romans 15:13 (NLKV), Paul prays a prayer for believers, and I pray the same prayer for you: "Now may the God of hope fill you with all joy and peace in believing, that you may abound in hope by the power of the Holy Spirit." Let me give you a picture of all the ingredients that are working together in the recipe for life that I have been writing out for you:

- **Hope** is the platform from which faith is launched. What we believe to be true and what we hope to see causes us to take a step of faith in that direction.

- When we encounter obstacles, time delays, struggles, and suffering, we have **patience**; we endure; we go the distance. Why? Because we know if we hang on and don't quit, there is a blessing and a provision of grace for us. Implementing the ingredient of patience and endurance keeps our faith out there working until it brings the desired result.

- We **worship** God in it all and count our blessings. Why? Because He's in control and as we hold onto Him and His promises, we will win. The end result? Even more hope. Your hope is even more alive than when you first stepped out on its platform.

Read these verses that describe it all. Romans 5:3-5 (NKJV): "...but we also glory (rejoice, count our blessings, and worship) in tribulations, knowing that tribulation produces perseverance; and perseverance, character; and character, hope. Now hope does not disappoint, because the love of God has been poured out in our hearts by the Holy Spirit who was given to us." The living hope we have in Christ will never be diminished. It is eternal, forever. Proverbs 23:18 (NKJV) states, "Surely there is a hereafter, and your hope will not be cut off." Romans 8:24a (NKJV) says, "For we were saved in this hope."

As a pastor, I have met a number of people who were so discouraged and in such despair that, in effect, they have said, "Pastor you don't understand. My life is two-thirds gone. I have wrecked so many things. It's too late to try to salvage anything that could make any real difference." I want to tell you that is a lie from the devil and that it is certainly not true. It is never too late, as long as you are alive. If there is still breath in your body, there is hope. Remember we are talking about a spiritual, miraculous, life bringing, life-changing hope that can perform the miraculous and turn it all around in just a moment of time.

Grace Wins

One of the most beautiful stories of grace in the Bible is the story of the thief on the cross. He had totally messed up his life, and now he was about to pay the consequences. He was being executed in the most brutal, torturous manner anyone could imagine: crucifixion. He was past all hope in this life. His life was being forcibly taken from him by others; it was out of his hands.   At least by earthly standards, it seemed too late for *anything* good to come from his life. The thief on the cross was all but history, a lost cause, beyond the reach of anything and anyone in the universe, except God. Yet in his darkest, most painful hour, with all hope gone, the thief on the cross was hanging next to the opportunity of a lifetime, a divine appointment with grace and salvation arranged by God. The man hanging on the cross next to him was none other than Jesus Christ, the Savior of the world, who was paying for the man's sins by dying on the cross at that very moment. As the thief on the cross saw and heard Jesus' prayer of forgiveness for those who were mocking Him and gambling for His clothes, he received a divine revelation of God's grace and forgiveness. Suddenly, he was flooded with hope, the living hope that only comes from grace. While others mocked, he believed. He cried out to Jesus and said, "Lord, remember me when You come into Your kingdom." Jesus turned and looked at the thief and said, "Surely today you will be with Me in paradise."

Not too long after He promised eternal life to the thief, Jesus cried out, "It is finished," as He died for the sins of the whole world. At that moment, He released into the world the most beautiful essence that has ever existed in the universe: God's amazing grace and undeserved favor. A few hours later, the thief breathed his last and died, but he didn't die a hopeless death. His heart was filled with hope, because he had experienced grace. Instead of falling into judgment and a Christ-less eternity, he stepped into eternal life. No more death, pain or sorrow. Just think of it! Grace took a man past hope—nailed to a cross—and made him the first and one of the most amazing examples of grace that has ever existed. In one moment, his worthless life became a very valuable life. Instead of being one of the nameless, forgotten ones, the thief stepped into the annals of history. He stepped into the pages of the Bible. He stepped into countless sermons and altar calls where people hear the story of God's forgiveness and gift of eternal life; how God can forgive them and give them eternal life. When I get to heaven someday, I want to meet the thief myself and thank him for the valuable picture he gave me of grace that I was able to share with so many others.

If you are reading this and you have not experienced God's grace, I would like to meet you on our website; I want to have an eight-minute session online with you called *Exit Strategy*. You can find it at rockfordres.org/exitstrategy. I will explain how you can exit your old lifestyle and your past and live a completely new life in God's grace. I will pray with you personally, and you will move into a new dimension of a life filled with peace and a sense of purpose that only comes from being right with God. I want to say it again: it is not too late for you. Christ is our living hope. Don't let discouragement or despair or hopelessness dominate your life. Identify that mindset and the thought patterns surrounding it. Reject them as the enemy's lies. Eject them from your life forever. 1 Thessalonians 5:8 tells us to wear the hope of our salvation as a helmet protecting our minds. God bless you as you engage in this whole process! You will find a true, living hope that can be totally realized, rising in your soul and motivating you to reach upward and onward, and nothing can stop that from happening. Romans 8:38-39 (NIV) says, "I am convinced that neither death nor life, neither angels nor demons, neither the present or the future, nor any powers, neither height nor depth, nor anything else in all creation, will be able to separate us from the love of God that is in Christ Jesus our Lord."

Pray this prayer: God, I thank You for the living hope that I have through Jesus Christ. Because of Your grace, I have eternal life and I have a purpose in this life. I reject hope-lessness and despair, and I choose to hope in You and the promises in Your Word. I ask You to help me build hope in my life by trusting and obeying You. I thank You, that You are for me and working in my life for my good. I thank You that nothing can separate me from Your love for me or Your purpose for me... in Jesus' name, amen.

Chapter 13 - Don't Waste Your Pain

Yet man is born to trouble as surely as sparks fly upward.
Job 5:7 (NIV)

As I come to the close of this book, I would like to review its theme and bring it to a conclusion in a way that you will remember long after you have finished reading. As I stated in the beginning, "the dark side of faith" is all the pain, trials, and trouble that you will incur in this life in your journey of faith. Jesus said, "In this world you will have tribulation, but cheer up, I have overcome the world." I have shared pieces of my personal story with you and I'm sure that you have a story as well. No matter what the dark side might consist of for each of us, the bright side of our life of faith is that God is using every trying circumstance that we go through to refine us and make us like Jesus. Further, He is orchestrating it all to position us to be in the right place at the right time to fulfill our mission in life, and do the work He is calling us to do.

You might remember the story I told earlier about a couple who lost their son in a terrible tragedy. The father had discovered his 23-year-old son Justin dead in a Michigan basement, overcome by the fumes of the special paint he was using. Justin had just gotten married 10 months before, and now he was gone—so abrupt, so cruel. To top it all off, this was the second son that this couple had lost. I felt prompted to go to their home early the morning after the tragedy and sit with them. We sat together, soaking quietly in pain. Finally, Paul blurted out to me, "We are so broken and hurting. We don't know what to do with it all. How do we go on?"

As I sat there, I felt the Holy Spirit give me a moment of illumination into their circumstance, and I said to them, "You are looking at this from the point of your pain and loss, and that is real, that is true, but let's try look at it from God's perspective. This moment, though agonizing and painful, might be the absolute mercy and grace of God at work. It just may be that He is allowing this to happen to do what is best for you and your son, in spite of all the tragedy." Previously, his relationship with God was questionable and shaky. Then when he went through pre-marriage counseling with his new bride to be, the minister at his church challenged him to have a living relationship with Jesus Christ. The young man prayed to receive Christ as his Savior, but from what I can recall, this young man's relationship with God was weak. He was not on fire for God and he was on the edge of beginning to drift back into some of his old friends and his old habits.

I said to his father and mother, "How do you not know that God may have looked down the road and said to Himself, 'this is the strongest point of relationship that this man will ever have with Me. He is in danger of drifting away. He is weak, but I love him, he is one of Mine, and I want to keep him in My grace, so I will not intervene and prevent his death. I will also use his life and his passing in My own unique way to build My kingdom for My glory and for everyone's good. It will cause momentary pain and loss, but it will preserve his soul and his parents will have their son as well—to share the joys of eternity together. No more pain, no more death, no more parting.'"

Even though none of us knew for sure exactly what God's will and intent was for that moment and circumstance, I want to tell you, something happened in that room. We all found a hole of Godly perspective in the cloud of despair that hung over us. In spite of all the pain, the parents found a mercy drop that can only fall from a provision of grace. Instead of being hurt and angry, the parents began to let it all go. They began to worship God and thank Him for His mercy, for grace and everlasting life. This always happens when we let go of our own very limited scope and reasoning, and trust in the One who holds the reins for this life and eternity.

A few days later, there was a large funeral. The father got up in the service and gave a moving testimony of the whole experience and then challenged young people to get right with God. As a result, a good number of young people responded and gave their lives to Jesus Christ. Meanwhile, the young bride who had lost her husband dedicated her life to God on a deeper level and later on took an interest in missionary work. Later on too, God led the couple who had lost their son into a grief counseling ministry that allowed them to minister in a special way to many who have experienced tragedy and loss. The father became an ordained minister. I spoke with the couple recently and found that they are planning to write a book on how to navigate tragedy and loss and let God use it for good.

As I said earlier, we will all experience trouble and sometimes even tragedy in this life, but I would encourage you to make the best use of it. Let it make you, not break you. In other words, ***don't waste your pain.*** Keep a God perspective for your life. Stick to Him like glue. Trust Him. Worship Him like Paul and Silas did in their pain in the jail. God made a way for them where there was no way. God will make a way for you too, no matter what situation, what crisis, or what circumstance you are in. Many times the purpose and reason for our circumstances may not be evident to us while we are experiencing them. Also, our expectations may take a real hit, because God many times does not meet our expectations; He has a higher, better plan that often is above and beyond our expectations. It's all about His glory, not our expectations. We must remember that we are co-workers in partnership with God. We are His representatives, building His kingdom on earth. Philippians 2:13 (NKJV) says, "For it is God who works in you both to will and to do His good pleasure." If you are experiencing things you do not understand and going through pain, discomfort, and trials that you can't see any purpose for, hang on to God, because He has promised in His word that He's doing something in you and through you, for His glory. It may hurt, but ultimately, He will orchestrate things in a way so they work out for His glory and your ultimate good.

God Provides a Way of Escape

I remember walking through a very difficult time with some good friends of mine. The situation began as Dave and his wife, Kathi, were sleeping peacefully in bed one summer night. They were awakened by masked men who were wielding knives. The men kidnapped Kathi and wrapped up her hands, feet, mouth, and eyes in duct tape. They demanded a large sum of money from Dave; they threw Kathi into the back of her SUV, and took off to an isolated spot in the country. They bound her to a telephone pole that stood in a huge cornfield in the middle of nowhere. Then they left her there alone, wearing only her nightgown. This would have been a terrifying experience for anyone, but in the middle of it all, Kathi began to pray in the spirit to God and reached out to Him for strength in her terror. She also meditated on scripture verses claiming God's protection. As a result of her prayer, she experienced a deep calmness, peace, and inner strength. God allowed her to keep her head and think clearly. She struggled and got free from her bonds. She ran through the cornfield to a back country road. Kathi heard God speak clearly to her about what to do next. She ultimately escaped, and about a week later her captors were arrested and charged with kidnapping. They were subsequently convicted and received lengthy prison sentences.

As you can see, God made a way for her in an impossible situation. He protected her as well, but something else wonderful happened in it all—since then, over a period of time, God delivered her from a good bit of fear she had struggled with in her past. She found a new level of confidence and security in her relationship with God. This prepared her for other serious challenges she has faced since. On top of that, her dynamic testimony has blessed and encouraged many others in their difficult situations. My video team produced a testimony video of her story which has been viewed (so far) by over 36,000 people. (You can see this story for yourself at our website: http://rockfordres.org/kathi). Recently, *Charisma* magazine, (a popular Christian magazine with a substantial subscription base in the USA), contacted Kathi and they are going to run her story of God's amazing deliverance in an upcoming issue. Her story of God's grace and protection has become an amazing, large platform from which she can share what God has done in her life with a tremendous number of people. Sometimes God delivers us from trouble. Other times, He allows us to go through trouble, but He always promises to be with us. In Psalm 50:15 (NKJV), God promises, "Call upon Me in the day of trouble; I will deliver you, and you shall glorify Me." Each aspect of the pain and struggle we go through in our lives—if we embrace it properly—will build something awesome in us and through us.

Training for the Next Age

There is one more aspect I want to share with you about the importance of embracing and navigating all pain, trouble, and hardship that comes our way. Everything we go through in this life is training not only for our purpose in this life, but also—and even more significantly—our role in the next age and eternity. Jesus Christ is returning soon, at the end of this age. In the next millennial age, Jesus Christ will set up an earthly kingdom and He will rule over the nations. He promised us in 2 Timothy 2:12a, that if we endure hardship, we will rule and reign with Him.

Revelation 2:26 (NIV) states another of many promises given to us in this vein: "To the one who is victorious and does My will to the end, I will give authority over the nations." The legacy promised us here is immeasurable. Our dark times and dire circumstances will not go on forever. We must do what Paul did. He saw what was at stake and he said, "I glory in my tribulations knowing that in it all, Christ's divine nature is being formed in me." We need to change our attitudes about our troubles in this life and see God at work in them, rather than complaining or doubting what His intentions are. We need to learn to praise God in the middle of everything no matter what, because we know what is really at stake. As we do so, we are looking beyond the moment, like Jesus did. Hebrews 12:1-2 (NIV) says, "Therefore since we are surrounded by such a great cloud of witnesses, let us throw off everything that hinders and the sin that so easily entangles. And let us run with perseverance the race marked out for us, fixing our eyes on Jesus, the pioneer and perfecter of our faith. For the joy set before Him, He endured the cross, scorning its shame, and sat down at the right hand of the throne of God." We are existing for a higher purpose and we are headed to a high-er plane and destiny. Ephesians 2:6-7 (NIV) states, "And God raised us up with Christ and seated us with Him in the heavenly realms in Christ Jesus, in order that in the coming ages He might show the incomparable riches of His grace expressed in His kindness to us in Christ Jesus." **This is the silver lining to a life of faith.** God's amazing future intent for us is to share the glories of Christ and rule and reign with Him in the next age and all the ages to come. **The core promise for the silver lining is** Romans 8:28: "...all things work together for good for those who love God and are called according to His purpose."

Embrace Your Race

As I close this book, I want to leave you with one last story. My friend, John Vereekan, along with his wife Karla, serves as the president of Global Outreach. He has lived and worked for 29 years as a pastor and a missionary in Mexico. He has labored and done groundbreaking work in Cuba and much of Latin America with John Maxwell and Marcos Witt, raising up and training thousands of nationals to reach their cities and communities with the gospel. If I were to think of one phrase that describes John, I would probably settle on "fast and furious." He reminds me of the Bible character Jehu. Jehu was one of Israel's Kings in the Old Testament. Jehu was an extremely driven person. When he was given a mission, he went after it as fast and dynamically as he possibly could. Similarly, when John came to Christ and married his wife Karla, they immediately went into mission work and set out to do as much as they could, as fast as they could, with all of their might. I have seldom seen anyone who put all their energies to work for one cause as John and his wife Karla did. Then something very interesting and unexpected happened in their lives. One of their children, little Timmy, developed viral encepha-litis shortly after his birth. He was severely brain damaged, blind, unable to talk, and unable to walk. In a way, his condition was worse than a death sentence; it was a living death sentence. John and Karla—and many others—prayed for a miracle. John fasted and prayed and said, "God, if You will heal my son, I will proclaim it for Your glory all over the world." John's faith in this situation was encouraged by the fact that he had seen miracles and healing in the lives of others in his ministry as a missionary, as I myself have.

But, as time went on, nothing happened. John eventually came to a crossroads. He came to the end of himself one day, walked out into a snowy field, fell back in the snow, and stared up at the sky. He could almost hear God saying "John, in this case it is not to be; trust Me." John had a real choice. It was, as he described it, a moment when one could shrink back from God, ask questions, and even wonder about the validity of everything they believed in and stood for. It was a moment in which one could feel alone, hurt and offended in that what they had believed for and hoped for and wanted so desperately, was seemingly being denied them. John said, "I had two choices: either lean out and shrink back, or lean into God." He continued, "I made a choice; I decided to lean into God. I decided to trust Him. I decided that no matter what, I was going to go the distance."

John and Karla didn't put their little boy in a home or an institution. They took full responsibility for him. They kept him at their side. Along with family and friends, they have cared for him and relied on the Lord for strength to do that and continue their task in ministry. That was 26 years ago. Here is what's amazing. John still loves life as much as I do—he is crazy for life. His marriage is rock solid. His wife, Karla, is pure dynamite—a spiritual giant—an example to any woman on the planet. Their ministry has influenced thousands of lives around the world. As my wife, Caryn, and I sat with John and Karla at lunch one afternoon and talked about all the challenges they had gone through, John said, "You know, Doug, if our little boy Timmy hadn't been in that condition and if I hadn't had to get desperate and dig deep and lean into God, I would've crashed and burned a long time ago, and we would not be where we are today." As I sat and listened to him, I suddenly realized God had done a miracle, only it wasn't with the little boy; it was in the lives of John and Karla. Through that very difficult ongoing trial and test, He had developed in them the ingredients of endurance and patience and a raw trust and dependence on God for strength on a day-to-day basis. It's the kind of stuff that turns a man and a woman into champions and world changers.

Someday soon, Timmy will be whole; he will be healthy. No more sickness, no more infirmity, only joy and endless celebration. No sorrow, no tears. Any pain he or they have incurred in this life will soon be forgotten, swallowed up in the joys of the next age and eternity. So I say to you again, *don't waste your pain*. Don't let it break you. Wrap your arms around it; squeeze all the life out of it you can, and let it make you. The Apostle Paul, after enduring some hard jail time and persecution for his faith, summed it all up in his epistle saying, "I am convinced that the suffering and light afflictions that we endure now, are not worthy to be compared with the eternal weight of glory waiting to be revealed in us." This life is short and fleeting. It's like a vapor that is almost insignificant when compared to timeless eternity. What we do and what we become in this life, though, will echo forever in eternity. I challenge you: live your life well and make the most of it. It's going to be worth it. The familiar song says it all: *"When we've been there 10,000 years, bright shining as the sun, we've no less days to sing His praise than when we've first begun."*

The End

Question to meditate on: What is the biggest challenge facing you in your life right now? Determine to see God's will and purpose in it all. Determine to do things God's way. Determine to go the distance. Determine to let what He wants to accomplish happen in your life. Embrace whatever situation you are in. Squeeze the life out of it. Let it shape you and mold you.

Prayer: God, have Your will and way in my life. Your kingdom come, Your will be done in my life. I believe that I will live every day that You've written down for me in Your book. I believe You have positioned my life for Your purposes in Your overall plan. It is perfect for me...I embrace the path You have set for me with all its joy and pleasures as well as any pain I might incur in doing Your will and being conformed to Your image, in Your likeness. God, make me like Jesus and get glory from my life. Your kingdom come, Your will be done in my life. Amen.

Prayer for Salvation: If you are not sure of your relationship with God and you want to get right with God and make sure you are walking in His plan for your life, I invite you to pray the following prayer:

God, I want to know you personally. I want to become Your child and a member of Your family. I admit that I am a sinner and I need Your grace. I believe Jesus died on the cross and paid for all my sins and rose again. I ask You into my heart. Forgive my sins and make me Your child. I receive Your grace. Thank You for coming into my heart. I embrace Your plan and Your will for my life, and I will follow You. I ask this in Jesus' name, amen.

Exit Strategy: I would love to spend some time with you and pray with you personally about your relationship with God. I encourage you to spend just a few minutes with me, while I share with you an Exit Strategy from the old way you are living now, to a brand-new life and a new way to live. Please visit rockfordres.org/exitstrategy.

Epilogue - Transforming Pain

Another kind of pain and discomfort we must endure is very unique to our walk with God, and that is sharing the sufferings of Christ. This is part of the process of walking in His steps and becoming like Jesus. On the cross, Jesus endured all the pain and suffering it would take to bring forgiveness to us all. As He hung there, He prayed an amazing prayer that let us and all of His executioners off the hook. He prayed, "Father forgive them, for they do not know what they are doing." Jesus suffered and paid for all the forgiveness that grace offers; then He gave that forgiveness to those who were unjustly causing Him great pain. Not too long after that, a follower of Jesus named Stephen was publicly executed for his faith by the brutal method of stoning. Even while he was experiencing excruciating pain, he followed Jesus' example. In his dying moment, as the stones struck him, he prayed loudly, "Lord, forgive them; do not lay this sin to their charge."

I recently heard an amazing story about a man named Amado Sarria. He was the head of a hitman squad for the Cali cartel in Columbia. He carried out so many executions that for a period of time it was said he ordered an execution before every meal. Eventually, Sarria's crimes caught up with him. He was jailed for attempting to ship over five tons of cocaine into the United States. While in prison, he sat helplessly in his cell and watched the live television report of his beautiful wife, Elizabeth, being gunned down by a hit man. She was shot a dozen times. Elizabeth had been his one true love. As he watched her body being carried out under a bloody sheet, he was overwhelmed by rage, helplessness, and despair. Shortly thereafter, a prison guard gave Sarria a Bible. As he read it day after day, his heart softened. He became a believer and follower of Jesus. Sarria joined the prison fellowship of believers and participated in the amazing transformation of Bella Vista prison. Bella Vista was one of the most notorious prisons in Latin America. It housed approximately 4,300 violent inmates, and an average of one murder per day occurred within the prison walls. However, as God's grace worked through the prison fellowship inmates, the entire climate of the prison changed. Instead of a murder virtually every day, the number dropped to about one murder per year.

Eventually, Sarria was freed and spent his time traveling to different prison fellowships, sharing his story of God's amazing grace. One night, after a meeting in a prison, a guard told Sarria that the man who had murdered his wife Elizabeth was in the audience, and wanted to meet him and ask his forgiveness. This was a defining moment for Sarria. He was a product of God's grace and forgiveness. He was traveling the country, preaching of the power that comes from receiving forgiveness. ***Now he was being required to give it.***

At first, he didn't want to meet with the man at all. He didn't feel like forgiving the man, even though he knew he had to. By now, Sarria was very familiar with one of the most somber statements Jesus made, which is found in Matthew 6:15 (NIV): "But if you do not forgive others their sins, your [Heavenly] Father will not forgive your sins." Jesus then proceeded to give an illustration of this truth by telling a story about a king who had a servant who owed him an insurmountable debt of ten thousand bags of gold. When the king saw that the debt was too large to be repaid, he ordered that his servant and his family be sold into slavery as payment for the debt. The servant begged for another chance, and the king had mercy on him and forgave him completely of the whole debt, and let him go free. In turn, that servant who had been forgiven went out into the street and met another fellow who owed him a hundred silver coins, which represented a very small amount of money. That person begged the servant for a little time to repay the small debt. But the servant would not hear of it. He threw him into prison until he would pay the last penny. When the king heard that the servant he had forgiven had not forgiven another person of a very small debt, he was furious and ordered that unforgiving servant to be thrown into prison and delivered over to the torturers until he would pay the last cent of his debt.

In this story, Jesus was pointing out the fact that we all have been forgiven for a lifetime of sins by God's grace and undeserved favor. Some of those sins we are not even aware of. Other sins were willful. Either way, God offers us all complete and total forgiveness and a clean slate. In turn, when someone wrongs us in any way, whether it is little or big, we are required to forgive them. If we don't, we stop the flow of grace and forgiveness in our own lives.

Sarria knew he had to face his wife's murderer. He said later that because of God's grace, they were able to hug and cry together, and Sarria forgave the man for his sinful act. Later on, he reflected about the experience. He said it was both beautiful and painful. He stated that in the moment of forgiveness, he experienced a unique, deep kind of pain not related to revenge or consequence. He said it must have been the kind of pain Christ felt on the cross as He suffered to forgive us all.

The Apostle Paul said something amazing in Philippians 3:10 (NIV): "I want to know Christ—yes, to know the power of His resurrection and participation in His sufferings, becoming like Him in His death." It can really hurt to forgive someone unconditionally, whether they deserve it or not. Our old nature is vengeful. It wants to strike back, hold grudges, get even. When we let someone completely off the hook, we feel the pain of our old nature dying on a whole new level. We find ourselves suffering for the ultimate good cause—identified with Christ—feeling some of the same pain He felt in providing us forgiveness. In no way is this partial payment for our sins, as some believe. But it is sharing in His suffering, which identifies us with Jesus in a whole new way. When we continually live a life of grace and forgiveness, extended to everyone from family and friends, to enemies, or just to someone who cuts you off on the road on the way to work, something is continually dying and something else is being renewed. Paul said in 2 Corinthians 4:16 (NIV), "Therefore we do not lose heart. Though outwardly we are wasting away, yet inwardly we are being renewed day by day."

I challenge you to stop at this point for a moment. Listen to God's voice speaking to your conscience and ask Him, "Is there anyone I need to forgive, no matter how big or how small the offense?" Decide to forgive them completely. Just like God forgave you. Let them off the hook entirely, whether they deserve it or not. Don't go by your feelings. Do this as an act of your will. Then pray for God to bless that person. Do this every time that person crosses your mind, until you know for sure it's all behind you. The pain we feel of letting someone go free is not wasted. It is good pain, with us sharing the same suffering Christ endured when He forgave us. Walking in this way is deeply transforming, and the end result is peace and freedom for us and everyone who crosses our path.

Study Review and Dialogue

Chapter 1: The Job Factor

Review and discuss how the enemy tries to separate us from our faith by using the circumstances of life to introduce offense.

1. We are given health, relationships, and material possessions that are often lost suddenly, or perhaps slowly, over a period of time.
2. We see the consequences of pain, sickness, estrangement, and death not only on ourselves, but also affecting those we love.
3. We pray for the desires of our heart, but our prayers are not answered in the way we would like to see.

Example
You were extremely optimistic about an area in your life: perhaps your profession, your marriage, your family, or

your education. Then, some things derailed and life threw you a curve. Something happened that you just hadn't planned on. You are finding that your hope in that area of your life has greatly diminished. You wonder, "Why did that happen?" You may even question why God allowed that to happen. Other doubts concerning your circumstances began to flood your mind as well.

What To Do

1. Recognize that the temptation to give up on God and become bitter is the oldest trick in Satan's arsenal. Refuse to focus on what you do not have, but rather all that you do have.

2. Consider the examples of those from the Bible who suffered great loss, but who still kept their faith and achieved spiritual victory, in spite of any temporary pain:

    1. **Job** (see *Job,* Chapters 1-42): Job lost everything except his wife, but he worshiped God through all of his loss, and God restored all that he had two-fold.

    2. **Moses** (see *Exodus,* Chapters 1-20): Separated from his family at birth and outcast from his society as a fugitive, Moses was led by God to a place of both earthly and spiritual leadership.

    3. **Joseph** (see *Genesis,* Chapter 30— Exodus, Chapter 1): Joseph had big dreams and was full of hope for his life and future. He was betrayed by his brothers, torn from his family, sold into slavery and forgotten in prison. Yet he clung to God and his dreams. Later, when his brothers apologized to him, he said, "You meant things for evil, but God meant it all for good."

For Group Discussion

1. Up to this moment, what has been the single largest trial or challenge in your life? What were the immediate consequences in your personal, professional, and spiritual life?

2. What are some of the domino effects from this event that continue to this very day?

3. When you experience setbacks, what is your support system (what enables you to navigate through it)?

4. Based upon your current understanding, how would you explain to a child the reasons why bad things happen to all of us?

5. Consider the psalm that David offered when he considered how thoroughly God was with him during all things, even death.

Psalm 23 (MEV)

The Lord is my shepherd; I shall not want.
He makes me lie down in green pastures;
He leads me beside still waters.
He restores my soul;
He leads me in paths of righteousness for His name's sake.
Even though I walk through the valley of the shadow of death,
I will fear no evil; for You are with me;
Your rod and Your staff, they comfort me.
You prepare a table before me in the presence of my enemies;
You anoint my head with oil; my cup runs over.
Surely goodness and mercy shall follow me all the days of my life,
And I will dwell in the house of the Lord forever.

Dedication

As you bring this first group discussion to a close, commit to one another that you will pray for each other during this time that God will heal any brokenness and will lead each of you to a place of understanding and healing.

Chapter 2: The Cosmic Wager

For Group Discussion
1. Why do you think that God engaged in a debate with Satan? What was His purpose in revealing that debate to us through this Biblical account?
2. The universal question at the heart of the cosmic wager between God and Satan was: will a man choose to believe in God, love God, and follow Him of his own free will, regardless of what happens to him? Or, will he listen to the lies of Satan and choose to go his own way? Discuss the fact that the same universal question that was at the heart of that cosmic debate still hangs over the head of every man and woman on the planet, even today.
3. When pain, trouble, and hard times hit, do you do you tend to look inward and blame yourself because of your inadequacy to fully please God, or do you tend to blame God? Have you considered that the cause of the distress could be for some other reason?
4. Discuss the fact that sometimes the difficult things we go through are not consequences or discipline for our imperfections, but simply a result of spiritual warfare that is going on behind-the-scenes, as God uses our lives, our decisions, and our actions to further His kingdom and disprove all Satan's claims and annul any hold he would seek to have on us.
5. Closing challenge: instead of being tempted to grumble or be offended by our circumstances and

troubles, consider the honor it is to be in partnership with God and His divine purposes. There is no higher meaning for our lives and our existence on the planet. Discuss the level of fulfillment and security that you have experienced from knowing that you are in the center of God's will and His purpose for your life.

6. Meditate on David's psalm about praising God through all circumstances.

Psalm 100 (MEV)

Make a joyful noise unto the LORD, all the earth! ²Serve the LORD with gladness; come before His presence with singing. ³Know that the LORD, He is God; it is He who has made us, and not we ourselves; we are His people, and the sheep of His pasture. ⁴Enter into His gates with thanksgiving, and into His courts with praise; be thankful to Him, and bless His name. ⁵For the LORD is good; His mercy endures forever, and His faithfulness to all generations.

Chapter 3: Don't Get Hijacked

Review and discuss the three steps the enemy uses to try to interfere with our thought process and lead us astray.

1. He begins by getting us to entertain a seemingly reasonable, innocent question of doubt about God or what God has said in His Word. Without realizing it, we adopt that question as our own thought process; then it becomes **our** question.
2. Next, the enemy inserts a conclusive thought concerning the question. You entertain and adopt it, thinking it is **your own** thought process.

3. The enemy injects an idea of a course of action you are going to take. You adopt the idea and path of action as a result of **your own** thought process. You have been hijacked and are now following the enemy's will and plan for you in that area of your life.

Example

You are plagued by thoughts of worry. You worry about everything. This makes you fearful about many things. This begins to affect your decisions and your actions.

What To Do

1. Recognize that these thoughts of worry and fear are from the enemy and decide to reject those thoughts of worry and fear as attacks of the enemy on your mind.
2. Put Godly thoughts in the place of your former thoughts. Google what the Bible says about fear and worry, or for that matter, any other area of your life: your job, your finances, or your family and future. Believe and embrace what the Word of God says about those things and do what it says, instead of what you have been doing.
3. Here are some examples of verses that you can claim and insert into your thinking process. If you believe these things and embrace them and think on them, worry and fear will become part of your past.

   a.   Matthew 6:34 (NKJV): Therefore do not worry about tomorrow, for tomorrow will worry about its own things. Sufficient for the day *is* its own trouble.
   b.   Philippians 4:6 (NIV): Do not be anxious about anything, but in every situation, by prayer and petition, with thanksgiving, present your requests to God.

    c.   1 Peter 5:7 (NKJV): Casting all your care up-on Him; for He cares for you.

4. Examine any area of your life where you may have been hijacked by the lies of the enemy. Identify it. Decide to follow the directive in God's Word con-cerning that area.

For Group Discussion
1. Share stories and examples of how your thought life was hijacked in some area.
2. Share how that thought or thought pattern affected your actions.
3. Share how you identified the problem and the struggles you went through to address it.
4. Share examples regarding how you are overcoming those problems and challenges and how that re-lates to the process we have just studied.
5. Pray the prayer of dedication over your thought life that the psalmist David wrote when he went through this same process.

Psalm 139:23-24 (NKJV)
    Search me, O God, and know my heart;
    Try me, and know my anxieties;
    And see if there is any wicked way in me,
    And lead me in the way everlasting.

I challenge you to pray this prayer from the heart for seven days, and periodically thereafter as the Holy Spirit leads. You will hear His voice speaking to you in your conscience. As you obey and follow His leading, you will quickly move away from the enemy's plan to derail you, into the center of God's plan for you. God bless you as you do this.

Chapter 4: Faith's Dark Side

For Group Discussion

1. The Dark Side of Faith is this: In your walk with God you may experience hard, painful things that have nothing to do with your comfort, your temporary welfare, your contentment, or personal gain; however, God is using these things as a necessary part of your life's purpose. How does this statement and the theme of this chapter impact what you have believed about God and His ways up to this point in your life?

2. As you reflect on your spiritual journey, how would you describe where you are right now with respect to your relationship with God? Share stories or examples of times when you had to examine and discard an attitude or idea about God and your relationship with Him.

3. Share stories or examples of people who have inspired you with their willingness to sacrifice their own interests for the benefit of others. In what context does self-sacrifice make sense?

4. Discuss the stories of the weavers and the airmen and the trust that these endeavors involve. Have you experienced relationships where you needed to have that kind of trust? If so, share a short experience from your life that illustrates this kind of trust.

5. If you had to describe "the big picture" of what life is all about in just a few words, how would you describe it?

6. Discuss the premise of John 3:16-17 and the promise of Romans 8:28.

John 3: 16-17 (NIV)

[16]And God so loved the world that He gave His one and only Son, that whoever believes in Him shall not perish but have eternal life. [17]For God did not send His Son into the

world to condemn the world, but to save the world through Him.

Romans 8:28 (MEV)
[28]We know that all things work together for good to those who love God, to those who are called according to His purpose.

Chapter 5: Why Does God Delay?

For Group Discussion
1. In the story of Lazarus, whose faith do you think was challenged the most? How do you think the series of events ultimately affected their belief in God?
2. Discuss times or situations in your life when you prayed for something and there was no immediate answer to your prayers.
3. When you pray for God's healing or intervention in the lives of others (whom you care deeply enough to pray about), how do you reconcile the fact that some prayers are seemingly answered, yet others are not?
4. Share stories or examples where you have seen the miraculous work of God in response to your prayers or the prayers of others.
5. Do you think God desires any type of response from us when we witness His miraculous answer to prayer? If so, what might that look like or involve? (See John Chapter 9, which tells the story of the man who was blind from birth and was healed by Jesus on the Sabbath.)

Chapter 6: A New Chapter

For Group Discussion
1. Discuss times and situations where you have felt a calling from God on your life. How did you know that it was His will? What seemed to hold you back or get in the way of you fulfilling that calling?
2. Discuss your current situation with respect to what you feel God is calling you to do. Is there anything in particular on your heart today?
3. In your view, what qualifies a person to do anything that God has called them to do?
4. As you consider those who have done tremendous things for God, what do you think makes them any different from you or me?
5. Discuss times or situations where you have been able to use the experience of negative circumstances or detours from your own life to help others and/or to advance the Kingdom.

Chapter 7: Amazing, Divine Timing

For Group Discussion
1. Psalm 31:15 says, "My times are in Your hands." When have you most felt that this has been true in your own life? What was going on in your life at that time?
2. Consider the story of Joseph, from the time that he was sold into slavery by his brothers until the time where he was placed in a position of authority, as second in command to Pharaoh. If you had been in his shoes, how long, or at what point, do you think you might have given up and come to the conclusion that God was disinterested in your fate?
3. In your own family, what situations, circumstances, or personal issues have deeply affected the fami-

ly and really challenged your family's unity? How have these situations been resolved?

4. What have you waited for in your own life, perhaps for a long time? In cases where you eventually have received what you desired, was there any benefit gained because of the period of time that you were forced to wait?

5. Discuss how God's divine timing relates to the times and situations where you are believing that you've done the right things to the best of your knowledge—and for the right reasons—but things still have not worked out.

6. Share times and situations where you have seen miracles of timing that went far beyond coincidence and could only have been brought about by the hand of God.

Chapter 8: A Recipe for Life

For Group Discussion

1. Psalm 37:5 says, "Commit your way to the Lord, trust in Him, and He will bring it to pass." How does this recipe for life differ from some of the other philosophies that you have heard being promoted by others who talk about how to succeed?

2. Discuss the directive in Philippians 4:6 that says, "Don't worry about anything, instead pray about everything." Talk about what life would be like if we did that to its fullest extent, which is what God tells us to do? What do you think is the main thing that tends to keep us from putting this philosophy into practice?

3. 1 Corinthians 2:16 says, "We have the mind of Christ." This means that we as believers have the same mindset and attitude as Jesus did. Go around

the group and share personal examples of adopting a God mindset in an area of your life, and how that affected your behavior.

4. Share times and examples from your own life where your solutions failed miserably, and things only got better after you let go and turned the situation entirely over to God.

5. What about peace makes it such a powerful state of mind?

Consider memorizing these verses where Jesus promises his peace to us:

John 14:27 (MEV)
Peace I leave with you. My peace I give to you. Not as the world gives do I give to you. Let not your heart be troubled, neither let it be afraid.

Isaiah 26:3 (NIV)
You will keep in perfect peace those whose minds are steadfast, because they trust in You.

Chapter 9: A Silver Bullet

For Group discussion
1. Metaphorically, firing a silver bullet means making a "can't miss" decision about what to do in any given situation you may find yourself in. When you do this, you win every time, and God wins every time. Example: Job experienced tragic, horrible circumstances that he did not understand at all. Although he didn't understand what was going on or why, he fired a silver bullet; he did the right thing. He worshiped God instead of blaming Him. Share examples from your own life where you fired a silver bullet—making a difficult right decision in a challenging

situation—and how God worked in your circumstances to make it a win for His kingdom and for you.

2. What is our only target when firing a silver bullet? (Answer: The will of God in every situation and circumstance). Discuss **WWJD.**

3. In 2 Corinthians 5:17, it says "Therefore, if anyone is in Christ, he is a new creation; old things have passed away; behold, all things have become new." If you are a believer, consider and describe at least one major way in which you are different now than what or who you were before you accepted Christ.

4. In Romans, Chapter 12:2, Paul tells us, "Don't be conformed to this world, but be transformed by the renewing of your mind." What is the practical method you can follow to accomplish this transformation and renewal of your thought processes?

Chapter 10: The Winning Mindset

For Group Discussion

1. Share a time from your own life when you were under tremendous pressure to cave in and do the wrong thing, but you somehow found the strength to withstand the pressure and do the right thing. How did things turn out?

2. Consider the story of Shadrach, Meshach, and Abednego, as they refused to worship a pagan god and faced capital punishment for their offense. Would the significance of their obedience be diminished if they had simply burned up in the fire, rather than being miraculously saved by God?

3. Discuss the idea that God can save you *from* the fire, *in* the fire, or *through* the fire. Even in the cases where the fire is figurative (rather than literal), which

of these three options is the obvious choice for how we would prefer to be saved? Why isn't this how it works every time?

4. In your own words, what is "the winning mindset" that is being discussed in this chapter?

5. "He gives strength to the weary and increases the power of the weak. Even youths and young men will grow weary and faint, but those that wait on the Lord will renew their strength and rise up on wings like eagles. They will run and not be weary and walk and not be faint" (Isaiah 40:29-31). Discuss how you are feeling right now. Are you tired and feeling faint, or do you feel strong, refreshed, and ready for whatever is coming your way? If it is the former, what can you do to trade that feeling in for strength?

Chapter 11: Go the Distance

For Group Discussion

1. Discuss the idea expressed in James 1, which says, "Dear brothers and sisters, when trouble of any kind comes your way, consider it an opportunity for great joy." In what way does this scenario make any kind of sense?

2. Share stories and examples from your own experience where endurance was the only factor that separated success from failure.

3. Discuss the importance of the fact that endurance is the ingredient that keeps your faith active and working.

4. James 1:4 states; But let patience (endurance) have her perfect work, that you may be perfect and entire lacking nothing." The Bible uses the words "patience," "perseverance," and "endurance" inter-

changeably. Discuss the different ways that this ingredient is so important in many different areas of our life, to the degree that it is the thing that *completes* us.

Chapter 12: The Final Ingredient: Hope

For Group Discussion
1. Discuss the current state of the world as you see it. What are some of the things that are real hope killers in people's lives? On a more personal level, what are some of the hopes you have for your own life, your family, and your community?
2. To the extent that you are hopeful of good things, what is the source for that hope (the confidence or optimism that these things will come to be)?
3. Discuss the idea that hope is a choice. Share examples from your own life or those whom you know who chose to exercise hope, even when there were difficult circumstances in their lives.
4. How does one go about building hope? What are the practical, concrete things you can do to bring real hope into your life?
5. Read Luke 23:32-43. Discuss the story of the thief on the cross and why God chose him to be the first example of the grace that was secured through Christ's death and resurrection.
6. Close by discussing the fact that any hope there is in this world can be traced back to the living hope that exists in the universe because of Jesus' death and resurrection from the dead that offers us eternal life. [I believe that even people who don't serve God have hope in their lives because they know if they want to, they can change; they know that there is an alternative. If the world was doomed and there

was no way out, there would be no hope in the universe, other than the fleeting anticipation of temporal things].

Chapter 13: Don't Waste Your Pain

For Group Discussion
1. Share examples from your own life or those you have known who have seen God bring something very good out of a very bad experience.
2. Consider the story of Kathi and her miraculous escape from kidnappers. Discuss and share examples from your own life where you were in a very sticky situation and somehow were shown a way through it.
3. Discuss the story of John and Karla Vereeken and their son, Timmy. What was the key to them finding the strength to face this long-term challenge?
4. The Apostle Paul, after enduring some hard jail time and persecution for his faith, summed it all up in his epistle saying, "I am convinced that the suffering and light afflictions that we endure now, are not worthy to be compared with the eternal weight of glory waiting to be revealed in us." Discuss Paul's perspective regarding the pain that we experience in this life.
5. What pain have you experienced in your life, either in the past or during this present time? Share ways you can see God working through it all.
6. What specific steps can we take to make sure that our pain and trouble is not wasted?

As we close our study of this book and its theme, I challenge you to meditate on an amazing statement the Apostle Paul made that essentially encapsulates the main message of this book.

Romans 5:3-5 (ESV)

3 And not only *that,* but we also **glory** in tribulations, knowing that tribulation produces perseverance; 4 and perseverance, character; and character, hope. 5 Now hope does not disappoint, because the love of God has been poured out in our hearts by the Holy Spirit who was given to us.

I hope and pray that each of you will find the strength to embrace, endure, and overcome with joy every hardship and challenge you're facing in your life, knowing that God is using it all to equip you, shape your character, and to position your life for His purpose and glory. God bless each one of you.

Romans 8:28 (NKJV)

For we know that all things work together for good to those who love God, to those who are called according to His purpose.

Epilogue: Transforming Pain

For Group Discussion
1. Have you ever wanted forgiveness from someone, perhaps even directly asked them for it, and they simply did not forgive you? If so, how did that make you feel? What consequences has it had on your peace of mind, your confidence, or your sense of self-worth?
2. Have you ever delayed in forgiving someone in your life? If so, what finally brought you to the point of forgiveness? What penalty do you feel you paid for delaying the forgiveness you eventually granted?

3. Along the same lines as having a "deathbed conversion," what might one lose by waiting until the very end of their own life to forgive someone, in what might be called "deathbed forgiveness?"
4. What type(s) of offense do you see as being "unforgivable?" Are there, in fact, any sins for which it might be seemingly impossible to forgive someone?
5. What part does someone's apology or regret play in your desire to forgive them? What role should it play?
6. If you have accepted Christ, how has His forgiveness affected you? How is your life different today because of it?
7. Have you forgiven yourself for the past mistakes you have made? What does forgiving yourself look like?
8. Together, pray *The Lord's Prayer*. As you pray, meditate on the power that your decision to forgive others has on the flow of God's grace and provision in your own life.

Matthew 6:9-13 (NIV)
> [9]Our Father in heaven,
> hallowed be your name,
> [10]Your kingdom come,
> Your will be done,
> on earth as it is in heaven.
> [1] Give us today our daily bread.
> [12]And forgive us our debts,
> as we also have forgiven our debtors.
> [13] And lead us not into temptation,
> but deliver us from the evil one.

About the Author

DOUG BERGSMA serves as the lead pastor of Resurrection Life Church in Rockford, Michigan. He previously served as a worship leader, Bible teacher, and elder with Maranatha ministries in Grandville, Michigan for 20 years. Doug also attended Christ for the Nations Institute in Dallas, Texas. He is happily married to his wife Caryn, and is the proud father of four sons and two daughters. Over a period of time, Doug became connected with Resurrection Life Church in Grandville, Michigan under the leadership of Pastor Duane Vander Klok. During this period of time, he participated in missions, crusades overseas, and worship recording projects. In 2002, Doug and his wife Caryn were led to plant a church in Rockford, Michigan. Since then, the church has experienced vibrant, explosive growth. Doug's sermon podcasts and the church's well-known transformation videos (celebrating stories of changed lives) are being viewed throughout the region and across the country.

Made in the USA
Middletown, DE
02 November 2015